ELIAS CANETTI

Party in the Blitz

THE
ENGLISH YEARS

Translated from the German by Michael Hofmann

With an Afterword by Jeremy Adler

A NEW DIRECTIONS BOOK

First published with the title *Party im Blitz: Die englischen Jahre*
by Carl Hanser Verlag, Munich, 2003. *Party in the Blitz* is published by
arrangement with Carl Hanser Verlag, Munich, and The Harvill Press,
Random House UK, London.

The publication of this work was supported
by a grant from the Goethe-Institut.

Jacket design by Semadar Megged
First published clothbound in 2005
Manufactured in the United States of America.
New Directions Books are printed on acid-free paper.

Library of Congress Cataloging-in-Publication Data:

Canetti, Elias, 1905-1994
  [Party im Blitz. English]
  Party in the Blitz : the English years / Elias Canetti ; translated from
the German by Michael Hofmann ; with an afterword by Jeremy Adler.
      p. cm.
  Includes bibliographical references and index.
  ISBN 0-8112-1636-5 (alk. paper)
  1. Canetti, Elias, 1905-1994 2. Authors, Austrian--20th
century--Biography. 3. Great Britain--History--20th century. 4. Great
Britain--Intellectual life--20th century. I. Hofmann, Michael, 1957 Aug.
25- II. Title.
  PT2605.A58Z47613 2005
  833'.912--dc22

                              2005019488

New Directions Books are published for James Laughlin
by New Directions Publishing Corporation
80 Eighth Avenue, New York 10011

CONTENTS

Party in the Blitz

OUT OF ENGLAND

I am confused about England, it was the whole of a life, inserted between a before and a since, and it would have been enough on its own.

After the chaos, I need to think what can be salvaged from such seeming order. Oh, what order. I was all ready to think: an order that would last for ever. And then, no sooner had the War been won, the victory celebrations, the bonfires on the Heath, than the collapse began. For a little while yet, people kept their wartime discipline. There was still rationing, but they were phlegmatic about it. It's a country where people like to grumble, but it's never serious—or so it appeared. It must once have been serious, when the religious wars broke out, back in the seventeenth century. I still can't quite bring myself to believe there ever was such a time, with so much agitation, and those wonderful eyewitness reports. A language that was derived from the biblical translations, or from the great drama. How tightknit was England then! Scotland was still Scotland, and Ireland only appeared to have been conquered. But the English were already putting themselves about on the seven seas, plundering from the Spanish, fighting the Dutch, beheading their own King—barely a year after the end of the Thirty Years War. How did that go together? Did the war adjourn to the island, the moment it was finished on the continent?

I think of the great poets after Shakespeare, who shared the seventeenth century with him: Ben Jonson, John Donne, Milton, Dryden, and the youthful Swift. And the prose of the first half of that century! Burton, Sir Thomas Browne, John Aubrey, I will never have read my fill of those men. Bunyan, George Fox, Hobbes—on his own, a titanic figure. How abject Germany looks by comparison! Spain better. France alright, but the greatest literature in that century was English.

And in the following century, it is still greater than all the others. In the nineteenth, likewise. But what happened in this century! I was living in England as its intellect decayed. I was a witness to the fame of a T. S. Eliot. Is it possible for people ever to repent sufficiently of that? An American brings over a Frenchman from Paris, someone who died young (Laforgue), drools his self-loathing over him, lives quite literally as a bank clerk, while at the same time he criticises and diminishes anything that was before, anything that has more stamina and sap than himself, permits himself to receive presents from his prodigal compatriot, who has the greatness and tenseness of a lunatic, and comes up with the end result: an impotency which he shares around with the whole country; he kowtows to any order that's sufficiently venerable; tries to stifle any élan; a libertine of the void, a foothill of Hegel, a desecrator of Dante (to which Circle would Dante have banished him?); thin lipped, cold hearted, prematurely old, unworthy of Blake or of Goethe or of anything volcanic—his own lava cooled before it ever warmed—neither cat nor bird nor beetle, much less mole, godly, dispatched to England (as if I had been delegated back to Spain), armed with critical points instead of teeth, tormented by a nymphomaniac of a wife—that was his only excuse—tormented to such a degree that my *Auto da Fé* would have shrivelled up if he had gone near it, drawing-room manners in Bloomsbury, countenanced and invited by the precious Virginia, and escaped from all those who rightly chid him, and finally exalted by a prize that—with the exception of Yeats—was bestowed upon none of those who would have deserved it—not Virginia, not Pound, not Dylan.

And I witnessed the fame of this miserable creature. I first heard of him—I didn't know his name—when I was living in Hyde Park Gardens in the very early days. Jasper Ridley, a young man just out of Oxford, married Cressida Bonham-Carter a few months before the beginning of the War, put me onto him with kindly condescension as the one, true poet, and "inducted" me by giving me a copy of his Elizabethan essays. A few years later, very young still, he died on the battlefield, and left Cressida a widow and their young son half orphaned. It is to this friendly, eager, open, cheerful, weak man, of whom I retain the fondest memory, that I owe the name of the driest figure of this century, of whom—later on, as the War ended, and he turned to the religion of his forefathers, only to give it up for that of the kings—I heard more and more, until finally there was nothing else.

That figure should have taught me what was happening to England. But the War intervened, the war in which England finally gave the world the best of itself, the first resistance against the maniac who threatened to stop at nothing. People have much for which to be grateful to this country, it cannot be left out of the essential story of mankind, any more than Florence, Venice, Athens or Paris. But the fact that in wartime I was delighted to receive its . . . made me unreceptive to the stink of enfeeblement that emanated from Eliot.

It is not in me to be luke-warm, least of all about England. There were slave owners all over, but where, except in the plantations of England, was there such an implacable urge to freedom? Where was there the refusal, the dissent, that began with the Quakers? Where did anything amount to more than conceptualisations, not Hegel, but not the pitiless emotional excess of Wagner and Nietzsche either?

The worst of England is the desiccation, the life as a remote-controlled mummy. It isn't, as people say, the Victorian (the mask of hypocrisy can be torn away, and there is something behind it), it is the prescribed desiccation, that begins with moderation and fairness, and ends up in emotional impotence.

In order to be absolutely truthful, I should have to track down every *needless* humiliation I was offered in England, and relive it in my memory for the torture it was; and then seek out every instance of sensitivity with which someone sought to save me from humiliation; hold them together, weigh them up, and have them cancel one another out, as happened to me.

Each thing, the one, the other, and both together, would amount to the truth.

Detailed memories that need to be re-animated:–

May 1945: the end of the War. The victory celebrations. The bonfires on Hampstead Heath. People dancing on Downshire Hill. My astonishment, my revulsion, my rapture.

William and Hetta Empson. Their parties, which were never like other parties, not least because it wasn't in Empson to keep quiet, because he spoke incessantly, at an extremely high intellectual level, and never listened to anyone not speaking the same highly cultivated language. In all the decades that I knew him and Hetta, and I lived very near by, this immensely intelligent man, one of the best and most eccentric experts on English literature, who had taught it in China and in Japan, and spent many years in the Orient, did not address so much as a single sentence to me that required an answer. Even today, I do not know whether he had the least notion who I was. Not long after the War, when a school of poets traced its descent from him (as a reaction to the exuberance and excess of Dylan Thomas), I would meet some of them at his parties, who knew my *Auto da Fé*, and took it seriously, and discussed it with me. He himself never saw fit to expend a single word on it, though he must have read it, he was a friend of Arthur Waley's, who never concealed his admiration for that book. I have no means of knowing whether Empson had the least idea of it. He read day and night, a thoroughly intellectual and literary man, Professor of Literature at Sheffield, as renowned for his books on literary topics as for his own poems. I often heard him speak, he had wit and verve, he was quick and confident, talked in streams of interpretative knowledge, very individual opinions and precise knowledge, perhaps the most fluent, inspired, clearest speaker I ever heard in England, among poets.

The longer it is since Mrs Thatcher left power, the gentler and kindlier my recollections of England. Things suddenly come to me that I was pleased to experience there, things that I liked about people who were sensitive and characterful. My vehement aversions didn't get any less, in fact with every memory, they seem to get stronger, I can't form the letters of Eliot's name without needing to inveigh against the man. Perhaps it was the ordering of his life that most irritated me about him, his early agreeing to live the life of the bank clerk, and later on his perfectly taken-for-granted directorship of a highly respected publishing house, which gave him power over the poets. Finally, his decision in old age to write plays for money, he never made any bones about the fact that that was what he was aiming at.

I never had anything to do with him personally. I only knew him very fleetingly. But, over the course of the years, I did often, at Kathleen Raine's, meet his Cerberus John Hayward, who lived with him in Chelsea, and through whose room Eliot had to go to reach his own. John Hayward was paralysed and wheelchair-bound, he was unable to get around by himself, it always required someone to push him. His face was distorted by a thick lower lip, whose red fleshiness it was impossible to conceal or reduce, and that gave his face a coarse, animalistic expression, quite at variance with the perfectly formed sentences in which he would at all times express himself. He had a thorough knowledge of English literature, in particular of poetry, and he edited anthologies of it that were well regarded. His affliction, his paralysis, set in, so far as I can remember, in Cambridge where he lived earlier, when he was a young man. It was lucky for him that when Eliot moved in with him when he went to Chelsea, that made him a sought-after character. Eliot did not go to parties, it was known that he avoided such occasions, but John Hayward loved to be asked out. Some young woman, usually resident in Chelsea, would be found to fetch him, his flat, unless I'm mistaken, was on the second floor, so he had to be pushed in his wheelchair to the lift, and driven down, taken out of the lift, trundled out into the street, and pushed to wherever the party was taking place. There was never a shortage of volunteers, in fact, there was a kind of vogue among pretty girls to be seen publicly in this helpful role. Since he loved parties, and loved talking to attractive women, he even had some choice, and was able to express certain preferences. In his conversations with people, he would invariably steer the subject to Eliot, and intimate that he was in a position to secure an invitation to tea with the great man. By offering such a prospect—however remote the chance that it might actually come to pass—he could win over anyone: people respected him still more than he deserved to be for his qualities as a critic, he was sought out at parties, sometimes people stood in line to present themselves to him, and he, knowing perfectly well that such enthusiasm was merely the result of dangling Eliot in front of them, did not scruple to dangle him a little lower.

Heath Street, Hampstead

There are the first years, up to the beginning of the War and beyond; then the time afterwards, in Amersham; and then the long later period in Hampstead. The periods are really quite distinct.

In the early years, you were a lost emigrant, happy enough to have come ashore, precariously through the War, to which you made no contribution, although you understood that it was directed also against you and yours. The wartime attacks on

London were at their height at this period. A certain courage—unconcern for personal risk—gave me back my sense of self. There was no need for you to offer to kill anyone. But you weren't a coward either, during those nights when much of London was in flames.

This period began in January 1939 and went on through the War till the autumn of 1941, when we moved out to Amersham, almost three years. Your relative distance from other emigrants, your first English friends, intense friendships with Franz Steiner and Kae Hursthouse. Steiner's being an anthropologist, and Kae Hursthouse a New Zealander, showed me something of the breadth of the English-speaking world; the crucial role that the Student Movement House on Gower Street played in all this.

Before: 1939, Hyde Park Gardens with the Huntingtons. Hyde Park Gardens. The first literary society I experienced in England, a party that was quite unlike any of the later English parties. L. H. Myers, who asked you if you had known Kafka. Philip Toynbee, who asked you the same thing. Talk about the Nazis, it was the time between Munich and Prague. War was in the air. Mrs Huntington, a tall, beautiful woman, who was married to the American director of Putnam publishers; the lift in the house, I was billeted on the top floor, in the room of their daughter Alfreda, my society really was the governess, a Swiss, who had already looked after me in Paris, a crowd of girls in Paris, each one more beautiful than the last. Without thinking about it, it was like being back in the Yalta, but surrounded by Englishwomen. Like Pinkie Esher's house. Alfreda was always especially cordial to me, I can't remember which room she stayed in after her return from Paris. She ran after me down the street once, when she mistakenly thought I was going to the

British Museum. A charming, idealistic girl, who wanted to do good in the world; she had a Van Gogh on her walls. But in fact I was not headed for the Reading Room, but for the Warburg Library. Ernst Gombrich, who worked there, had introduced me. It was on a recommendation from his mother that the Huntingtons had taken me in. The Warburg allowed me to borrow books as well.

It was *Mr* Huntington who was unpleasant to me as soon as I set foot in his house. He asked me whether I had lived in a flat or a house in Vienna. He was surprised to learn that I had a wife living in England as well, I told him she was staying with her brother in Surrey. He asked me what her brother did, and I replied: "He is a small businessman." That hardly applied to Bucky, but I sensed Mr Huntington's snobbishness, and was ashamed to tell the truth. Bucky, married to an Englishwoman from Manchester, was an innocent, well-meaning, rather insignificant man, really a sort of Charlie Chaplin figure, who had already tried all sorts of things in an endeavour to keep himself, his wife and their little boy afloat. In Manchester, he had had a barber's shop. For some years now, he had had a little sweet shop in Lightwater, near Bagshot, Surrey. I was too cowardly to go into detail. Nor would Mr Huntington have cared to hear it, so I said, "He is a small businessman," or I may even have said, "He is a very small businessman," and I'm not sure whether I said his name, Calderon, or not.

The governess, Miss Hübler, was always strict, as she was used to the company of the girls she was trying to turn into young ladies. The great moment in the lives of these beautiful creatures was their presentation at Court. Alfreda's was to be later that year, and when I talked to Miss Hübler in the nursery next to my own room, we would of course talk about that. It was my first introduction to elevated English circles. The other, much more exciting, was a few minutes away, at Hyde Park Corner, where I went on all my free evenings.

England feels very remote to me. I haven't been there for five years now. It's starting to become an island again, an island in the memory, it's on its way to becoming transfigured, already I'm beginning to dream of visiting it, as though it were something from early childhood. I was eighty-three when I was last there. Many things you don't understand in the way they presented themselves to you first. What has it become entangled with now?

What suited me to such a degree that it settled where I would least have expected it? Party political feelings, fed by the newspapers, are the most detrimental. They were always crude, and remain so. But there are other things that were never affected by partisanship, and for a long time remained, so to speak, unmentioned. If some of *that* surfaces, then you should grasp it right away: it blossoms quickly, and withers away even more quickly.

I began by talking about William Empson, to whom I was always a stranger, because it was a friend of his wife who introduced me into the house. The Empsons had a large house on Haverstock Hill, most of it was let. Hetta, who came from a South African Boer family, was an unshakeable Communist in her convictions. She was a very beautiful woman, and the people she brought into the house were one of two sorts. Either they were intellectuals of any colour and provenance to whom she felt drawn by her politics. She turned over all the flats of the house to them, with the exception of her own quarters. Her lovers, of whom there got to be quite a number over the years, she sometimes even allowed into her quarters. Empson seemed not to have anything against it at all. He had a sharp, active, ramifying literary intelligence, schooled in the Metaphysical Poets of the early seventeenth century, but also in the Cambridge school of linguistic sociology (I. A. Richards). His mind was always running on such matters, everything else he left to Hetta. You had the impression, coming to the house, that each of them had their own life, without getting in the way of the other, and respecting everything to do with it, even if it was diametrically opposed to whatever he or she thought. Empson himself struck me as completely asexual, it was a little perplexing that there were two boys from that union, who grew up in the midst of their mother's tangled love life, without coming to any apparent harm from it.

When they gave their very generous parties, friends of each of them would come, bringing friends of their own. Things were really quite lively and free of vanity and formality. It was possible that a very famous poet might have been there for a couple of hours, holding exciting conversation with Empson, and no-one else took any notice, yes, no-one else even knew about it. There was no fuss made of the person of the guest. He was not dragged around in that "European" way and introduced to everyone, nor was he left in a mysterious nimbus of privilege and arrogance. He was there the same as everyone else was, and if he happened to interest Empson, then there was a lot he could talk to him about. But if he didn't interest Empson, then he might leave the party as discreetly as he had come, and most often, you wouldn't even learn that he had been there.

In my recollection, those were the only Hampstead gatherings of any size that took place on their own account, and not to reconfirm an existing pecking order or, alternatively, to facilitate possible climbing. They were never boring, you always ended up talking to someone who had had some interesting experience, or who was genuinely odd. But nor could you complain about not being anyone yourself, that remained my own situation in England for decades, and even in the last years, it only superficially changed. I enjoyed Hetta's benevolence, she was a good friend of Friedl's, she liked people, and she was a very tolerant person.

Her political views, attributable to her upbringing among Boer zealots and their black serfs, were quite unshakeable, but they did nothing to limit her as a person. Her benevolence aside, for a long time I encountered nothing else in that house. A lot of emigrants came, famous ones, unknown ones, ingratiating ones, proud ones, I was one of them, small distinctions among them didn't interest the master of the house, whose passion was for English poetry and English literature. Their foreignness didn't strike him, he was preoccupied with a far greater, truer foreignness, in which he had lived and taught for long years of his life: Japan, China. Perhaps he learned some Chinese—though I can't quite believe it. His thinning hair he wore like a Chinese sage. I still have the feeling that right through his Chinese period, which politically must have been tremendously exciting, he remained the man I saw later on in England, marked by the rhythms, the vocabulary and the passionate intellect of early English poetry.

So I was condemned to complete impotence with this man. It would never have occurred to him to talk to me about the Chinese masses. I would have been burningly interested if he had, but what would he have had to say to me? It would have appeared to him like small talk, which he despised.

So I went gladly enough, but still somewhat shamefacedly, to the Empsons'. You were asked along, but for Empson it was as though you didn't exist. There were a lot of people there who didn't exist, but there were a lot of the other sort too, who did. Neither the one category nor the other conferred any sort of distinction.

NO-ONE IN ENGLAND
OR
THE SILENCE OF CONTEMPT

You could describe it as an advanced social training. You're brought together into a small space, very close, but without touching. It looks as though there might be a crush, but there isn't. Freedom consists in the distance from your opposite number, even if it's only a hair's breadth. You move smartly past others who are crowding in on you from all sides without brushing any of them. You remain untouched and pure. It would be accounted a fault, a stain, if you permitted yourself the least contact with anyone else. A tall upright man, unable or unwilling to twist and squeeze past others, lets others do his twisting and squeezing for him. An individual's identity is expressed by an active form of restraint. Its crowning version is when it doesn't show itself as such. Anyone who is so famous as to be generally recognised doesn't really belong in a party, unless he is such a master of disguise that he manages to make himself completely invisible.

An ideal situation would be if a great many people came together, among them a fair number of people one knew, but who themselves gave no indication of the fact. The riddle of mystery and distance mustn't shrivel, otherwise the party would collapse like a punctured balloon. As soon as too many of those present know one another, the state of aggregation of the whole would change, and continence would turn into a rather banal form of friendliness. The condition of not-knowing supplies more tension, especially if you know how important it might be to know this man or that. The urge to climb in society is always alive, it is fuelled by reverence for the very highest echelons, but tamed by the difficulty of approaching them, and, even if an approach has been successfully made, then by the difficulty of touching them. This is something only learned in closest proximity to others.

It is taken for admirable modesty if very prominent persons mingle with others and succeed in distinguishing themselves so little that they remain unrecognised. They wear no masks, but nor do they introduce themselves. You can have a conversation with someone, without having a clue who he is. He can walk away from you, without having the least sense of obligation to you. Nothing has been promised, nothing transacted, it was an innocent exercise in espionage, that suppressed any thought of . . . The one mustn't sense how deeply he is despised, and the other mustn't let on how much power he would have anywhere but here.

Because, of course, power has accrued, but it has been distributed as well, and . . . its limits by being concealed in the midst of so many others. It is not so soothing to those who have it, if it encounters equals, and gives itself to be recognised. It remains—out of forbearance so to speak—in concealment, so as not to frighten those far less powerful than itself. The letters that people have after their names to signify the degree of their prominence are not worn, and only gradually become visible in the course of a conversation. Often the man conversed with is left behind, in a condition of bafflement, racking his brain: "Who was that? Who can that fellow have been?"

Be mindful of proportions. Aymer, Gavin and their mother are still far too much in the foreground for me. Probably because of the travels I went on with Aymer, which have amounted to considerable parts of my life. I want to think more about the others, and draw them out of their shadows.

I have barely touched on anything to do with Veronica Wedgwood. I am reluctant to publish the true image of her I have. Once, she was the first Englishwoman who with enthusiasm and belief, took up the cause of *Auto da Fé*. She put time and work into the translation. Also, she was very taken with Friedl, and particularly by the nature of the relationship she had with me: as the student who loves her teacher, and willingly allows herself to be formed by him. Later on, Friedl disappointed her, by her life, and by her occasional dependency on her. The widespread rejection of *Auto da Fé*, which actually was relative—even then that book meant a lot to certain people—and the claim of *Crowds and Power* when that finally appeared, and which she tried to help with a very positive essay, but never really read, my awful disappointment when it dawned on me that she did not really *know* the book at all, that it had not made her want to *read* it, even though she had heard so much about it over the years, and—and this was the limit—her enthusiasm for Mrs Thatcher, which she came out with as a historian—she saw that government as a new Elizabethan Age—all that makes it practically impossible for me to discuss her truthfully and in detail. There would be so much to say about her, so much that she confided in me, I cannot do it, I seem to hear her warm, almost flirtatious voice, I can see her father ahead of me on Leith Hill, I liked him from the moment I met him; her arrogant mother, who disliked her because she never wanted a daughter, and who remained a source of nightmarish oppression for Veronica all her life. These things that were really the essence of her I cannot speak of; I do not think much of her own writings, she was unoriginal, had no ideas of her own about anything. But she liked writing, and she was industrious, she read sources, letters, documents, diaries, her curiosity was really quite insatiable, though not insatiable enough, and above all: she adapted her thoughts to some prevailing stream of thought, whether it was political-historical or psychological. Since I very rarely have any regard for historians—particularly those of our age—I am not really in a position to say anything about her in the way of a judgement of her work. All I can do is record personal traits of hers, moments in the garden on Downshire Hill, while we were discussing the last chapter of the translation, and Friedl was looking down on us from a first-floor window of the house, and anon brought us some tea. It was Veronica who stubbornly insisted that Jonathan Cape publish *Auto da Fé*. To begin with, there hadn't been any idea that she would ever translate it. I had thought of Isherwood, because I liked his Berlin book. It was only with great hesitation that Veronica approached me with the idea that—with my help—she might translate the book herself, and, with the proviso that it not appear during the War, I finally agreed. My life's work was *Crowds and Power*. I didn't want anything of mine to be set before the public until that was finished. Nowadays, I would describe that as a rather self-denying ordinance, perhaps a type of guilt *vis-à-vis* those who, whether they wanted or not, were gathered up by that war. It was to oppose the increasing speed of developments that I hoped to push this patient investigation, there wasn't a moment . . . that I undertook in those years, there was a quite unshakeable conviction that I had to get to the root of things. There were terrible lessons with which I saw myself confronted, the more terrible as there was never the least *hurry* about them. They had time to spread out, and put down roots. In the early years, Veronica had some understanding of that process. We often talked about English history, the seventeenth century was her real subject. She knew a lot about it, and talked to me about it, and that encouraged me to read up on it on my own. When I tried to explain the various mass movements, of which at that time there were many in England, she was quick, almost brusque, in her attentiveness. Her capacity to absorb things, the way she absorbed them, was her real strength. She had nothing of the sluggish reserve of so many English people. She traced her descent to Celtish ancestors, she herself was dark, and really most un-English physically. Her father had the face of a Celtic magician, a "wizard", as I used to say to Veronica. He was in charge of one of the great English railway companies, his real interest was history, his library contained practically everything that Veronica wanted to read on the French Revolution. He had been friends with Joseph Conrad, who often called, Veronica remembered him from her girlhood, and she was able to tell me a lot of things about him that she had heard from her father. Her uncle was Josiah Wedgwood, a Liberal of the old school, prepared to speak in Parliament on behalf of any cause that seemed to deserve his advocacy, he was like one of those men who, in the history of the nineteenth century in England, were every bit as real and as important as their rivals, the ones who built the Empire.

I was genuinely fond of Veronica. I relied on her. She had the warmth that I missed among those English intellectuals I knew. She fascinated me, furthermore, with her extended family: the Darwins, the Wedgwoods, Macaulay, Trevelyan, Francis Galton and Leslie Stephen, Virginia Woolf's father. They were all related; in the intellectual history of mankind it would be difficult to find a comparable family.

Perpetuation of arrogance: it's taken over by those who have no title to it. Their life devolves to a single effort: to get their arrogance accepted.

Veronica was free of such arrogance, perhaps because her mother, who thought herself entitled to it, pursued her with feelings bordering on hatred. Kathleen Raine had little else but that drive.

Kathleen Raine was a poetess inasmuch as she had found a dramatis personae and an emblem for her pretension: the two sunny boys on the bridge next to their mother.

It is an easy matter to mock pretensions, if you think you have heights of your own, which haven't been challenged.

The modest air of most of the "highest" English. Dinner at Diana Spearman's. The juridical fluency, politeness, but also vagueness (if one didn't matter) of a Maxwell-Fyfe. A striking example of the highest English cultivation was afforded me by Francis Graham-Harrison.

Francis. Always close to me, he was formed by Eton and Oxford, and perhaps equally by a cultivated father, who was a legal adviser to Parliament. Francis had absorbed Classics at Oxford, but also philosophy (Austin). He knew a lot, and was passionately interested in books. It was possible to discuss some thousands of titles with him, so long as one didn't get into too much detail. He was helpful, accommodating, but still insisted internally on certain immovable principles of justice, tolerance and scepticism, in accordance with the English tradition. In the person of his mother, he had experienced the further reaches of faith: intolerance and condemnation. In his eyes, which were like those of a persecuted beast, there was something very affecting: a revulsion against the weapons, sport, physical culture, etc., that constitute such an important part of an English upbringing. I don't believe he ever tried to change anyone's mind. He was a diligent civil servant, and, with his intelligence and so on, he was forever being promoted to higher and higher grades—you only got to hear of it by chance. He was party to the enthusiasm of others, and not only women. Anyone who spoke out with confidence, understanding and taste gripped him, particularly women, who set about their aim with confidence. He was helpless before them, he contrived things in such a way that they approached him and identified in him a willing prey. He was seduced, and he was true to any seductress, I mean to say, she could repeatedly seduce him over long periods of time, if she liked, even if there were others in the meantime, who did the same. This way of winning women by concessiveness I was able to observe in him more than in anyone else I have ever known.

On the nearness and distance of the English.

Distance is a principal gift of the English. They do not come too near. They may not, they cannot come too near. For their own protection, the person sheathes itself in ice. To the outside, everything is patted back. Inside, you're left to freeze.

Social life consists of futile efforts at proximity. These are as hesitant as the person making them is brave. He really is, because he knows how alone he truly is.

Basically, you shrink back from anyone new: you fear in him the worst, someone who will leap over the distance you set up. He may give every appearance of reserve, but you do not trust him, and keep him off with elaborate politeness: the silent, but searching question with which you investigate him, "How high? How low?" is as existentially important as it is implacable.

For the Englishman, calm and self-control are the only legitimate ways of getting through life. Anything encompassed in other ways must be done on a grand, piratical scale, to meet with their approval. The robber is a feared, but, from childhood on, also a popular figure. It is almost always possible to find a set of noble motives for him. Even if he fetched up on the end of a rope, he was greatly popular, the role of the gallows is profoundly important in the social history of England. Swift says it with unforgettable dispatch: "And swing he shall!" he says in one of his letters to Stella, in which he's also talking about his increasing influence on the Minister. It's not a dramatic case, but something that would later have been accounted a sexual misdemeanour, for us something ridiculous, slightly obscene for him, but fun: "And swing he shall!" he concludes with delectation. The pleasure at the swinging back and forth of the corpses can only be compared to Beatlemania.

So people came together. But petty occasions—someone had stolen a loaf of bread, someone else a pair of socks—caused hardly any delight, it had to be a proper robber, who had all manner of lives on his conscience. What mattered was that he had himself committed murders in the course of his robberies.

The protection of the person, its solidity and security is not an easy matter. How much of that distance has remained in English life?

I am only able to comment on the wartime and the period

after. During the war, the tautness of this distance relaxed, people got closer to one another, people even—miracle of miracles—spoke to strangers on the train. Of course, the usual chitchat about the weather preponderated, but there were occasions when something else followed.

What most deeply impressed me was the time of the catastrophes: when England was all alone, and battleships were being sunk. One could not help feeling a faint stir of unease on the top of a London bus, after the latest sinking had just been announced. The odd mouth opened, it didn't say anything, but even so, it didn't immediately fall shut either, it remained open for half a moment. Sometimes sentences were spoken. Expressing contemptuous courage. Never, not once, did I overhear an anxiety, or even a complaint. The worse things stood, the more determined people were. Perhaps there weren't many who saw the danger in its full extent. But no-one was flippant, and no-one really blind either. The unequal nature of the fight was common knowledge at the time. The enemy was given almost affectionate diminutives: "little old . . ." That did not mean any more than that people knew who he was, and what his game was. An enemy wasn't just an enemy: you also had to take cognisance of him. There was something in that conferral of the status of enemy that was then immovable.

Probity. It has something to do with the law, but spoken, not written laws. English speech gets lazier all the time. The emphasis of governesses: Mrs Thatcher's case exceptional only in the context of Parliament. You can say all you like, she'll still come back at you. Men either as craven or as young thrusters. Diana Spearman, a far more cultivated person altogether, was an earlier instance of the type for me. Thatcher is a respecter of the existing structures, but the top one, the one to aspire to, is that of wealth. It starts there—the nauseating indifference of wealth, that, as a parvenue, she has in her blood.

Did I know people like that? Most comparable was an émigré from Frankfurt, from a family of wine growers.

The Scots: drier? Less dry?

All of it obscured for me by a figure I knew too well, stupidly well, in the way that an analyst might know someone: I'm talking about Carol—where my willingness to listen led to a dependency, a craving, and at the same time an insight into the family, to every generation.

Really, it was the foreigners who were more interesting, particularly in their frantic attempts to become English. You have to draw a distinction here between the enormous, gigantic, ubiquitous literature of England and her power. Everything has got so tangled together, that it's easy to be unfair. The "little" war over the Falklands, which was "accepted" by most people, is like a final memory of power, in that it cost lives—a certain number of lives. The main part of the exercise conducted in ships, the most dastardly thing the sinking of a ship. It is impossible to say how many memories were roused up and down the Atlantic by this mini-war. Helpless dreams of the past, in people who never fought: invalids, women, pacifists, everyone, people of every sort, not just veterans, they all, or a lot of them, went around with happy little smiles, when there was talk of that "memo". In reality, it was the satyr play of empire, and I never got over it. I, an Englishman by attachment, loving it twice over on account of Veza's enchantment with the place, never got over my embarrassment at this mini-war: England's version of the Colosseum, war games out to sea.

My yearning for English words, written down, I have to say, begins to preoccupy me. In particular it's for words as a summation, reduced formulae, words that earlier used to repel me, practical words like "busy", "fuss" and "ready" now excite my admiration.

I cannot get over my astonishment at the terms that Swift already used to collect. (He was like Karl Kraus, much earlier, and much better.)

I recite Blake's poems in utter ravishment, they mean even more to me than German literature. There is an exuberance there, no less than there is in the young Goethe. It's true, there is no English Hölderlin, but there is everything else, *and better.*

When I talk about England, I notice how wrong it all is. I mustn't talk about England any more, the only English experiences of mine that are still valid are poems and sentences, and most of all: words. Words bob up in front of me, they must have been the most ordinary words of that time, and they appear to me to be so beautiful, so remarkable, so insightful, that—quite without there being any context for them at all—I simply fall in love with them.

There, and only there, is the fruit of what I have written about England, the fact that words can find me again. Maybe it's to do with the fact that I haven't used them for years. Maybe the words have a sense of lying idle, and come to me with renewed purpose: here I am, I'm still around, more than ever I am there; see me, make use of me.

AMERSHAM

I t's a sort of idyll, but in a state of wartime. Every English eccentricity and peculiarity represented, the religious ones too, which are unrivalled the world over. One can describe it all calmly and without rancour. It's especially amenable to memory, because it has no consequence. A lot of old people, who will never change. The mild landscape, a real paradise. Friends of two types: refugees from Europe (émigrés) and evacuees from the bombing in London, which is only an hour away. Chattiness on the train, in the beechwoods and farms. Old towns built along rivers. Old cemeteries. People, "humours" as represented in literature from Dickens back to Ben Jonson. Oxford and its learning only an hour distant.

The most advantageous thing of all is the position of the writer, who counts for absolutely nothing here, an unknown and a stranger, but, because of the whiff of Vienna, perhaps someone to confide in. It's possible to tell him things one wouldn't dream of telling one another.

I sometimes think about Friedl now. I saw her in front of me in the woods between Fingest and High Wycombe. That was during the War, in 1942. Fingest, a beautiful village, a side of England I like to think back on. I like thinking about England in wartime. I had a great respect for people then. It was a general

Friedl Benedikt

respect. Even though I might hold different views on individuals, I will not have anything said against them as a people. I did not have any respect for the pilots who flew over us night after night, and came back a few hours later, without their bombs. There were lots of women, whose husbands were away. But there were women in the Army too. There were old people as well, where we lived, living all alone in the big houses, not at all eager to take in people from the city. There were priests, the tiniest of hamlets had one. There were fugitives from many European countries, they too evacuated a second time from the city, where they were in danger. We were living with a vicar, a peculiar character I'd like to write about. In Chenies, this place very close to Chesham Bois, where we were living, there was a vicar who wrote books on the history of religion and knew about snails, Smith was his name. When we were expecting a visit from him to our minister and it had been raining, he would arrive—this was a sin for the English—late, because the rain would have brought out the snails, and he picked them all up and inspected them one by one. He did not have any choice in the matter, he was a connoisseur and a lover of snails. If they were out on the paths, then he would be late. His face was like a soft, spongy mass, and I only understood it once I realised he had got it from the snails. His face was as naked as a snail's body. In a house not far from ours, there lived another gentleman, Mark Channing, who had spent many years with the Army in India. He had approached the . . . of the Indians and written books about India that were widely read. He lived with a girl he called Ariel, who had to dance for him from time to time. He had a heart condition, and had to avoid any sudden or strenuous movements. It must have been doubly health-giving when the girl danced for him. He died while we were living there, and was cremated, in accordance with his wishes. I called on Ariel, as one does, to say some comforting and friendly words to her. She was very pleased, held out his ashes to me, and asked me to touch them. She asked if she should dance for me. I said no.

I knew a lot of people there, and have plenty of things to say about them, but I notice I'm just beginning to forget their names. These were people I used to see in the street every day over several years. Some I visited in their gardens, others you met at a musical evening, once a month. Some invited me to their homes, others told me funny and moving stories. I try to reproduce their names, I can only manage with a few, and yet it is not even fifty years since life pitched me in their midst. Mr and Mrs Crovo—it was Mr Crovo I spoke to on my very first visit to Amersham. I did not know my way around at all, and had come to see Marie-Louise, who had just moved out there with her mother. On Chestnut Lane, I met a man with a round, blond head and bright eyes, not at all old. I asked him the way to Stubbs Wood, which was the road that Marie-Louise and her mother lived on. He offered to show me a shortcut through his own overgrown garden, through all sorts of shrubs and bushes. He was very chatty, on the way he asked me where I was from, his English sounded vaguely accented. When I told him I was born in Bulgaria, in a place called Rustchuk on the Danube, he was very surprised, because he was a Romanian himself, and came from Giurgiu, just across the Danube. He had been an oil engineer, and came to England in his early years. There he had married an Englishwoman, who owned property here, and had lived here for decades now. He deduced from my name that I was Sephardic, and was unable to refrain from telling me a Jewish joke, but so dressed up that I could not be directly offended. This had never happened to me in England, because there was a war on against people who behaved like that. He enjoyed our encounter, led me around for a long time through the shrubbery, it cannot have been a shortcut, and finally, the moment we found ourselves in Stubbs Wood, pointed out the house of Miss Meakin, where Marie-Louise and her mother were living.

Mr Yetts—the ex-sailor and Sinologist. I believe he went on to become Professor of Sinology in London.

He couldn't speak German, and asked me to read a book of Franke's about the (Han Dynasty) Confucian Tung Chung-Shu, and give him an English account of it.

• • •

Veza Canetti in Marie-Louise von Motesiczky's studio in Amersham

Mr Falconer—an Egyptologist, pupil of the great English Egyptologist, Alan Gardiner, who wrote the Egyptian grammar from which ancient Egyptian was taught at that time, Friedl's uncle, married to her Viennese aunt, Heddi.

Falconer had been in the Army as well. He was particularly interested in the Egyptian military. He wasn't a worldly man like Yetts, he seemed rather folksy, like the gaiters he always wore. But there were occasionally lectures at his house, and he showed good reproductions of Egyptian funereal art.

Miss Brailsford—from an old Quaker family, who wrote history books. She gave me a monograph she'd written on James Naylor. A small, frail, very ancient woman, with a wobbling head. Her brother was:

H. N. Brailsford—the celebrated journalist and author. He was a very old man when I met him. He had once reported on the Balkan War for the *Manchester Guardian*. He was one of those well-informed and thorough journalists *The Times* and the *Manchester Guardian* used to employ in those days. Among his other Balkan interests, he had been interested in the Sephardic Jews, and had picked up for not much money on a barrow an old account of the history of the Turks in Rycent. This book is very important, because it contains a contemporary account of Sabbatai Zvi. Brailsford *gave* me this book, for no other reason than that I was Sephardic. It was the oldest thing in my library, and probably very valuable. Much later, I gave it to Gershom Scholem, when he visited me in Hampstead.

Musical Evenings—every month, at Eric Newton's mother-in-law's. At the centre of the music was Francesco Ticcioti, a pupil of Busoni's. But there were all sorts of talks as well, on painting, literature, philosophy.

The German woman who was married to Colonel Sparrow—she had previously been married to a senior S.S. officer in Germany. She divorced her husband—or did he die?—and somehow met Colonel Sparrow, who married her. I don't know any further details of how the relationship came about. She had a baby by him, an infant when, in the last summer of the War, the newly invented German rockets, the Flying Doodlebugs came along. One struck the Sparrows' house near us in Chesham Bois, and killed the child. The mother felt personally persecuted by the Germans for her desertion, and was close to madness. It took a long time, half a year or more, before she recovered from the blow, and adopted a couple of coloured babies.

The young red-haired actress and her mother—they were spiritists, the daughter painted, and was visited by the spirit of Jan Steen. She thought she painted according to his instructions. Those Jan Steens are really something to see.

We went sometimes to the Repertory Theatre in Old Amersham. It was the time of Priestley's plays, which were written under the influence of Dunne's philosophy of time.

The bookshop—Mr Milburn buys Eliot's *Four Quartets*, for a shilling each. He panics about the price when he gets home. He presses them on me, lest his wife see what they cost.

Old Daisy—and Kathy her daughter. She and her father deliver milk on their little cart. The mother is sick. She has depressions that last all winter. All this time she is bedridden. From time to time we hear her roaring. In spring, she improves. We are able to visit her. She shows off her flowers, and the big cherry orchard, everything that never changes. I forget the family name. They're on Chestnut Lane, the oldest farm in Chesham Bois.

Mrs Lancaster, the Irishwoman—where Veza lived for a time. Her ghastly husband. Her fancy man, the old grocer.

"DURRIS", STUBBS WOOD, CHESHAM BOIS

Mr Milburn played a great part in our lives. We lived in his house in Chesham Bois, when we moved to the country from London. The bombing raids were coming thick and fast, the War looked bad. The Germans went from conquest to conquest.

When I presented myself in "Durris", in Stubbs Wood, Mr Milburn was sitting downstairs in the living room with his wife. There was a grand piano in the room, she had once given piano lessons. She was quite as religious as he was, you could see her innocence written in her face. The lank white hair drooped over her long face, her eyes were opened wide as for prayer. Her timidity dated from that greater part of her life, in which she was alone. From a prophetess who advised her, she received the vision of a man who lived with his books in an ivy-clad cottage in the New Forest. Miss Slough, the prophetess, whom I later got to know quite well, did a good turn to the pair of them, when she showed them images of their desolateness, and persuaded them that they would do better to live together.

Mr Milburn, whose first name was Gordon, was even skinnier than Mary, whom, once a week, under particular circumstances, he would call Agnes. His hair was still thinner than hers. His face had deep vertical furrows, perhaps from study, he had studied all his life. A little goatee beard was the

Mrs Milburn, Amersham

only pert thing about him. He was very friendly when he learned that we were émigrés from a German-speaking country, and from Vienna at that. Perhaps he imagined that we had been through harsh experiences, which was hardly the case. Where victims of persecution were concerned, he had a Christian heart. He showed me the rooms upstairs that we might live in, one of a normal size, a living room where Veza could also sleep, and a tiny bedroom for me. It was a town full of gardens, each one more attractive than the last, outside our windows were a couple of large poplar trees that he pointed out to me. "They won't take away your light," he said, "you'll be able to write here." He quoted some incredibly cheap figure for the rent, we could have lunch with them, his wife cooked vegetarian meals. She wanted to say something, but he wouldn't let her, and said with all the kindness of which he was capable: "You know, I scribble a bit myself." I felt how much he wanted us to come. The authorities were exerting pressure on householders in the area to take in people from London. If they did not find anyone by themselves, then lodgers would be found for them, which was not always agreeable. Some big houses were lived in by single old gentlemen, or, more commonly, ladies. It went against all common sense, to leave such premises almost empty at a time when more and more people were trying to get out of London. Mr Milburn was happy enough to have found tenants without children, and—even more—ones who asked if they might bring a few books with them.

For our part, we were equally happy. The rooms were pleasant, bright and clean, and the garden stretched away down the hill. It was how I had always pictured country living in England. Mr Milburn, who had been a vicar, seemed no longer to exercise his calling. I tried to imagine the sort of books he might possibly write, and assumed they must be religious tracts, but that was only partly true.

The very next day, we moved in. Mr Milburn welcomed us in a sort of dither of happiness. He was so thin, that I was surprised he had room for any such vestigial feelings. But I was wrong on this aspect of our moving in. He welcomed us without any reservation, and had astonishingly few regulations for us at the outset. There must be an endless number of things one mustn't trespass against with him, but he did not mention them, he wanted to be kind to us. His wife was a little alarmed by Veza, who could not repress the fire in her countenance, and straightaway began talking about the bombing in London. Mrs Milburn cared neither to talk about such things nor to listen to them. "Evil is not really there," she said mildly. "Evil is a projection of ours." "What about the bombs?" asked Veza, ignoring my desperate efforts to get her to keep quiet. "The bombs are imaginary," said Mrs Milburn. At last Veza noticed my signals, and desisted. She had misinterpreted them, and thought I had been indicating that Mrs Milburn was mad or, strictly speaking, feeble-minded.

As far as our lunches together were concerned, it seemed to be a bad start. But once we were alone again, I was able to convince Veza. We were dealing with a completely innocent person, who could not imagine the evil of which people are capable. Veza would end up feeling sorry for her, I said. Because since evil—during this war—was all too patently there, she would reach for Satan, and curse him as a dangerous

Anne's Corner, Chesham Bois

enemy. This happened in such short order that Veza, who wasn't easily impressed in these matters, expressed herself impressed with my understanding of human nature. We got to hear a lot about Satan in the coming weeks. He was everywhere. He had set up quarters in every pub. Mrs Milburn would often appear outside the nearest pub, which was a five-minute walk away, and, in little speeches, warn the drinkers, in little speeches, who stood around outside with their glasses of beer in their hands, of the bad impression they were making.

Later, when we were exchanging a few confidences, Mr Milburn admitted to me he was concerned when we got ready to move into his house. He did not take us for alcoholics exactly, but Mary did not permit a drop of alcohol in the house, and on Veza's first fiery outburst, she had voiced the suspicion to her husband that she had been drinking, and was perhaps even of Satan's brood.

But, in spite of the rural peace round about, there was war, and it was almost baffling how people who were so afraid of evil that they either claimed it didn't exist or else attributed it to Satan personally (and went back and forth between the two views)—it was baffling how they dealt with the War. Mr Milburn took the *Manchester Guardian* daily, a very good liberal newspaper, and was keenly interested in world affairs, he hated Hitler and his war. It filled him with satisfaction that good and evil were so clearly identified in this instance. Not for a second did we doubt, he or we, which side was in the right, and, still more, which was in the wrong. Wrong took on more forms, and it was also much more animated, because it came directly from Satan. But, at the time we moved into the house, it was impossible to ignore the fact that the wrong was everywhere in the ascendant and that an attempt on the part of the Germans to invade was by no means ruled out.

Most of all, Mr Milburn was consumed by an appetite for prophecy. He had the deepest respect for prophets. Apart from the Evangelists, those were the parts of the Bible that he was continually reading. He never claimed to have a prophetic gift himself, but he needed it and sought it in others. From time to time, Mr and Mrs Milburn were visited by a prophetess, who regularly made the rounds of all her believers. They lived scattered all over the country, and the prophetess needed to have recourse to the bus for her visits, and fearlessly undertook one- or two-hour rides. Miss Slough, that was her name, Lily Slough was a large, fattish woman with a swimmy but still forceful and expectant look in her eye. She reminded me of pictures of shamans that I had seen in books about the peoples of Northern Siberia. But I never experienced one of her prophetic fits, they happened downstairs, in the Milburns' drawing room. I only ever got to see her upstairs in our rooms, each time she came to the house, she would first call on us upstairs. There, she would shyly quiz me about the state of world affairs. Her questions, hesitant to begin with, soon became precise and astute, she was a good listener, she noticed any discrepancy, and did not rest until it was properly cleared up, and nor did she ever make any attempt to prophecy anything to us, that is Veza and me. On the contrary, I had the feeling that she needed people like us, who seemed to be up on current affairs, for her prophesying. Like everyone else, I suppose, I had certain hopes that I nursed, to try to get me through the anguish all around. I reached for any straw, there wasn't much in those days, and was rather surprised to hear what became of them. After an hour with us, Miss Slough would go downstairs, where Mr and Mrs Milburn would be waiting for her with bated breath. And then she would duly have her "fit", which lasted barely half as long as the time she spent up with us. She left the house in a kind of trance. I watched her go, walking down the gravel path from the house, stiff and upright, she never looked back. I was certain she could feel my stare. But she knew she could not turn round to give me a cheery wave, because Mr and Mrs Milburn would be standing by the window of their room downstairs, not taking their eyes off her either, till she disappeared from view.

At lunch, which we always had together, we would then get to hear an exact account of Miss Slough's predictions. She had used everything she had gleaned from me. Nothing was left out, I recognised the drift of her questions, and was astonished to have relayed back what I had said by way of reply to them. It was all raised into biblical language, the driest facts sounded feverish and mighty. All doubt was banished, and I began to believe myself. Even things I had said barely an hour ago, tentatively enough, now sounded as though they had come from the mouth of Isaiah. The two listeners weren't able to give things back with the fire with which they had heard them pronounced, but their emotion, especially Mrs Milburn's, who was quivering like an aspen, made up for what they lacked in the way of force. Miss Slough must have spoken in a state of unimaginable exaltation, one of her fits saw them through two months. When uncertainty began to return, she would reappear at exactly the right moment. Veza was indignant at what, with some reason, she thought of as deception. But I sensed that she, like me, harboured a certain admiration for the quickness and nimble-wittedness of this woman, who was entirely uneducated, and, even though she was hearing some names for the first time, used them with aplomb. We were shy of admitting as much to one another, we had reason to feel ashamed in front of the other, but the prophetic speeches as they were rehearsed to us by the Milburns, had a certain effect on us as well, though we knew every detail of their provenance.

You must also consider that all of this, the information as much as the ensuing revelations, was in English. At that time I was getting to know the prophetic books of William Blake, one of the most wonderful poets in English, or any other language. I do not think I would have ever truly grasped them without my experience of the wholly un-intellectual Miss Slough.

I might also add that Mr and Mrs Milburn also owed a considerable debt to her. They had each lived alone to quite an advanced age, she as an anxious tormented music teacher, he as a vicar, who had renounced his post for religious uncertainty, and had retired to a remote, ivy-swathed cottage in the New Forest. Mrs Slough was already acquainted with them both, and visited them separately, at a time when they didn't know of the other. It occurred to her that it might be better for both of them if they lived together, and she was able to communicate to each the vision of the other in their solitude. The cunning with which she went to work, the certainty of her images, would be worth a precise description. This I cannot provide, and so must content myself with saying lapidarily that she was the onlie begetter of their marriage, and that neither of them could have endured to live with anyone else.

It is a moot point whether Mr Milburn was ever capable of emotion. At the time I met him, there wasn't the faintest trace of it. He knew it, and longed for nothing more. Before I describe how he and I went looking for his feelings, I should like to illustrate the extent of his inner petrifaction. He was avaricious in a way I have never come upon before or since. He would allow himself nothing, nor anyone else. A torment for him at the time were the public collections at that phase of the War. Among these there was an "Agricultural Red Cross Fund". Like all his neighbours, he promised to set aside a penny a week towards this fund. The man with the tin came every Monday between ten and eleven o'clock. Mr and Mrs Milburn always got up early, to make the most of the daylight hours. I could hear Mr Milburn trotting briskly about, up and down the stairs, out into the garden, then back into the house, till at about ten to ten he vanished down the gravel path. He was gone for some time, I assumed he had gone out to the shops, which were some distance away in town. Shortly after ten, the man came calling for Mr Milburn with the collection tin. I paid the penny for him. He returned after eleven, and vanished into his study. Before lunch, I would tell him the man had been round for the collection. He was very relieved, and thanked me profusely. This would happen one Monday after another, until I finally realised that for two hours every Monday he stayed away from the house, so as not to have to cough up that single penny.

Out of gratitude, then, Mr Milburn told me a lot of his history. He had been out to India as a Church of England clergyman, and had spent many years teaching at a mission school. Gradually, he had begun to doubt the Thirty-seven Articles of his faith, until eventually his doubts became so strong that he was forced to leave the Church. Then he embarked on a search for a new faith, he went from sect to sect, certainly for more than half of his long life. He stumbled upon the most startling things, each of which took him in its grip, and he would follow them for a while perfectly submissively, until they turned out to be wrong, and filled him with fury. Then he would roundly condemn what suddenly struck him as a swindle, and turn towards some fresh variant of belief, from which he hoped for salvation. Gradually, I was able to piece together his story. I took a course from him on the English sects, so to speak, and there wasn't one that was missing, they were all there. You may say that he changed every other year, as it were, moving house, settling down in them, and even though, as I said above, he had a total absence of feeling, this craving for religious housing never left him. He didn't make it easy for himself, and would go through all the principles of whichever deviation it was. In his study on the ground floor, looking out on to the gravel path that led up to the house, he wrote incessantly. The room was littered with notebooks full of his writings. Sometimes he succeeded in luring me into this room. Then there would be no escape, and he loaded me up with a dozen manuscripts that I had to take back upstairs with me and read. He wrote in a sober and unmetaphorical English, in which statement followed upon the heels of statement, each one stiffly enumerated. It was a little like reading a long list of book titles, but without the pleasure in their variety. It was the driest thing I had seen in almost forty years of life. I was so full of revulsion at this writing, that with blind intensity, far stronger than I had ever experienced, I threw myself upon what had always fascinated me: the pre-Socratics and every sort of ethnic myth I could lay my hands on.

On such occasions, I would hear from Mr Milburn what principles of what sects were oppressing his conscience. His conscience was as inexhaustible as his feelings were atrophied and withered. Whilst in India, he had become interested in the Upanishads. To understand them better he had learned Sanskrit, and translated some of them into English himself, and published them, one of the few books of his authorship there were, not that anyone was aware of it. In India, this was clear to me, he had sought a universal feeling, in the hope that at least he might find such a thing. But even in India, he had rapidly come up against what was in his nature: discriminations, separations, sharp distinctions. So the Upanishads could not quench his thirst for feeling either, and he gave up on them too, without however condemning or decrying them. What never failed to astonish me about him was the richness of the sects he had tried out. He pulled on each one like a jacket, and then took it off again, he didn't throw any away, he kept them all, just as if they had been old clothes, I think that was the source of his avarice, the fact that he could never bear to part with any of the beliefs he had ever worn. Perhaps he had the secret modest hope that out of some mixture of all of them, the one true one might be produced.

He described the prophetesses who had been to his house—he was much more suspicious of male prophets. Emily, a woman he had only met much later, had an adventurous life behind her. She had joined the retinue of a Persian, a magnificent specimen, with a mighty black beard, a handsome mystic who travelled all over the world, and filled auditoria wherever he went with speeches of renunciation. A group of well-off ladies, of whom Emily was one, formed a sort of praetorian guard for him, and since each of them was equally remote from him, as an ascetic, there was never the least jealousy among them. As part of this retinue, Emily had been to all the great cities of Britain and America. One day she saw him backstage, just as his show was about to begin, with one of the praetorians on his knee, and was so astonished, that she fell into a dead faint, and had to be carried away. When she came to, she decided she would make amends for her sin. In every one of the cities she had been with him, she hired the hall in which he had spoken, and conducted impassioned denunciations of the seducer. She reproached herself for having failed to see through him, and, standing on the same spot where once he had stood himself, warned his former audiences against him. As she had money, she was able to assuage the pangs of her conscience within a couple of years. She left out none of the cities where they had been together, and, with, I believe, one single exception, she always managed to hire the same hall as the one in which he had spoken.

Only then did her anguish abate, and she turned to the Adventists, where she witnessed a wonderful act of prophecy. The return of the Lord was to be expected within a few years, and it was known where he would first set foot on the earth. It was on a hill in Cornwall, which she purchased on the spot, so as to be on hand for the Resurrection. With that, Emily's narrative broke off. Mr Milburn had known her at the time of the purchase of the hill, and she had told him with great agitation of the incident with the Persian. She was bathed in tears when the contracts were exchanged for the hill in Cornwall. She had asked Mr Milburn to be there to witness the transaction. He had watched her throughout, and, as he admitted to me a little shamefacedly, had envied her her tears.

That was one of his most positive spiritual experiences with sects. There were others, though, and if I were to report on all of them, it would make a book of unimaginable richness. There is nothing that people have not believed, nothing for which they have not hoped. I must force myself not to continue. It is no part of my purpose that people give up all hope.

As may be imagined, Mr Milburn was undaunted by any obstacles, except where money was involved. As I say, he had already learned Sanskrit, and he had studied German as well. That was at an earlier, more conventional, time in his life, when he was content to read established theologians and ecclesiastical historians. There were many Germans among them, and he read them in the original.

But he also had a secret wish, which he had harboured for many years. I was not a little astonished when shyly he broached it to me, in beseeching tones. At the time he was learning German he had tried to read Hölderlin, and had not understood it. Would I be prepared to read and explain Hölderlin to him?

Would I be prepared! I was delighted. It was to remain a secret from his wife. I gathered, without quite understanding why, that he felt vaguely guilty for cherishing such a desire. At the bottom of the garden, as it rolled down towards the valley, there was a big oak tree, with a wooden bench and a table under it. There, you were out of sight of the house. The grass was so long, it was so far from the house, you couldn't even hear if someone was calling for you.

So there I sat an hour a day with Mr Milburn, all summer long, and—there's no other word for it, I'm afraid—"did" Hölderlin with him. While I read, his features changed. He was as tense and expectant as a child. This dried-out man, whose face was wholly made up of wrinkles, glowed. I had always asked myself earlier what he had done with his eyes. He never once interrupted the course of a poem. I had the feeling he did not understand any of it, but was listening with great concentration. At the end of a poem, there was silence, as though he was afraid to disturb the moment with his scratchy voice. *I* had to be the first to speak. I did what I like to do least of everything in the world: I started to explain the poem to him. Ordinarily, I would never have forgiven myself, but here, under these circumstances, it was the right thing to do. He took it as the commentary on a sacred text. I started to get a sense of why he incessantly made his way from one such text to another. None of the Greek bothered him. He took the names of the Greek gods in his stride, as though they'd been references to the Christian god. I think the array of names was a kind of salvation to him. I wasn't ashamed for one moment. I never apologised to the poet for my explanations, which otherwise I would have done.

So with this man, I "did" Hölderlin every day for many weeks. Aeroplanes flew over the garden, we were of the then already mistaken view that some of them were German. As I will go on to say, there was nothing that frightened him more, he was almost as frightened as his wife, whom we called "the aspen". I don't mean to poke fun at his Hölderlin bliss. But he felt protected by it. He didn't attend to anything but the words of the poet. Once he looked up, he had heard loud engine noise, assumed it was a German plane, and said: "Maybe the pilot has a copy of Hölderlin in his pocket." I lost the thread and did not reply. I thought, He is trying to forgive the people of whom he is most afraid, he is the most avaricious man I know, and yet—for this one moment—he's a Christian. I am perfectly aware of the misuse to which I put Hölderlin, but I do not regret it, because none of it was lost on me.

I stand by this militant statement, which may appear dreadfully inappropriate. I am not ashamed of it. I know what other people were going through at the same time. And I know too what miserable things I went through with those two people, during the years we spent in their house. I know how much Veza—who was never able to put on any pretence—suffered from them. But always before me I have the poetry-transfigured face of Mr Milburn.

At the time of our stay in "Durris", Stubbs Wood, sirens often went off. Mrs Milburn, who had very sensitive hearing, would tremble all over. "Gordon, where are you?" she would wail. They would quickly find each other, he took her by the hand, and briskly walked her into the kitchen. There was a large square kitchen table, stout and immovable, on strong legs. Not letting go of each other for a moment, the two of them would slip underneath it, and lie side by side beneath its protective canopy. They were quiet as mice, so as not to attract any attention, one assumes they must have lapsed into prayer, as it seems they always did, only on this occasion, silently. Gradually, thanks to Veza, they calmed down. In these situations, Veza was never afraid. She simply didn't have the time, because there were always other people around whom she had to protect. She went calmly back and forth in the kitchen, which at other times was off limits to her, fiddling with pots and pans, and preparing lunch. If it took a long time, the Milburns would get hungry. They never actually said so, their fear lest a pilot's attention be drawn to them by their voices never left them, but when Veza set their lunch in front of them under the table, they lapped it up as avidly as dogs. The sounds of their eating could be heard even up in our quarters. As dogs, they need have no fear of the bomber pilots. Only people had to get out of sight. I would go down to the kitchen, I could not miss out on such a spectacle. They felt Veza's presence as protection, and it was augmented by my silently joining her. It was hard to believe the two skinny people trembling under the table, and yet eating greedily. It seemed almost incredible to me, in this country where I never once saw people, women, children afraid, even when they were in real danger, even when the City was in flames. Then, whatever had to happen happened in complete calm. Children did not scream, women were never hysterical. Everything was anticipated, everyone knew what to do, and when a bomb fell, help was promptly available.

When I watched the old people under their kitchen table, almost motionless for hour upon hour, but eating quite brazenly, when I felt slightly ashamed that I had to watch, but also felt proud of Veza who did the one correct thing, and gradually calmed them down by getting them something to eat, when I think about the situation now, fifty years later, and the other three no longer alive, it becomes clear to me what Mrs Milburn was afraid of: divine rage. That was fixedly before her, and with it she also infected her husband, who wandered from one faith to the next, and certainly was not always waiting for divine rage. But Veza was immune to fear if she was able to save others from it. When she was alone with the visions of what was going on all over Europe at that time, she suffered the pangs of hell. "Would you like to swap with the Milburns?" I asked her once, as she was just going about her business, and sat exhausted on a chair. "Why not?" she said. "It wouldn't hurt to *really* know how other people feel, instead of just imagining it. But I wouldn't be capable of *eating*. No-one could force me to do that."

Veza was very embarrassed by my "teaching" Hölderlin to Mr Milburn. That was how she referred to it, and once she went so far as to "mislay" our book.

THE STREET SWEEPER

The street sweeper in Chesham Bois was a stout old fellow, with a round red face and a fringe of white hair. He looked like a fresh-painted apostle. He seemed to come strolling out of a painting that was perfectly familiar, although *he* somehow wasn't. We used to see him always at the same corner, where a footpath branched off Chestnut Lane to Stubbs Wood. He would be calmly sweeping, as if there was all the time in the world, propping himself on his broom, and looking doughtily ahead of him. He would look everyone in the eye who came up, but greet only a few. Fewer still were graced by his conversation. He would be the one to begin, it would have appeared odd to make a start oneself, because his work as street sweeper might have suggested he was someone to be condescended to. But that was out of the question with this self-evident apostle. People of his type sometimes sit for painters, but in this case it would have been inappropriate to think of such a thing. On the corner of Chestnut Lane, there was a small general store, and even though there was not much to buy there in wartime, people went there to collect their rations. For such a small village, there was quite a concentration of people, all brought there by the little shop.

The street sweeper looked at them all closely, and he knew every one of them. It wasn't simply on account of his age that he was the veteran of the quarter. He had a slow way of looking, and thought nothing of fixing his regard on someone for a long time. It would never have occurred to anyone to suspect him of curiosity. But that's precisely what, in his fashion, he was. The first time I emerged from the store, I felt his look levelled at me. I felt it at my back all the while I was going round the corner. What did he see, staring after one like that? To have him look you in the eye seemed as natural to him as his white fringe of hair. But then he would stay to watch the movements of the man whose face he had stared into. I always felt well when I was around him. At first, I thought it was to do with the fact that he came from another world, where there was no talk of war. But that was wide of the mark, because, after I had known him by sight for a long time, and yearned—really, no exaggeration—to have a conversation with him, after passing him so many times, without daring to speak to him, the longed-for moment came about in the most natural and yet surprising way. He asked me if I had heard the news that day, and wanted to know what I thought about it. He spoke slowly, with perfect enunciation, in a language I would otherwise have described as biblical. And yet it was about current events, about bombers, tanks and battleships. He was well informed, and knew more than what he could have gleaned from the news. Without offering me any particular courtesy, he set me apart by asking me his question, because he hoped to learn something from me. I knew that he spoke to others on other matters. About the children who had been evacuated to the countryside, about the peaceful night, about the local beechwoods that had just recently been cut down. He surely couldn't know anything about me because, apart from Mr and Mrs Milburn, none of the locals had met me. Now he said to my face: "I know you read a lot, there's something I don't understand," and then came his questions. Many of them were so intelligent that I was unable to answer them. But that didn't annoy him, and I sensed rather that he liked me for it. It was the most lucid conversation I had ever had in this place, where I lived for several years. It was picked up again; each time I passed, he greeted me in the most cordial fashion. Our conversation continued as though we had spent the intervening time thinking about it, and wishing to take it forward. His speech showed me that he read his Bible a lot, it's written in the most majestic English. He never quoted from it, however, yet he also indicated that he had read the diaries of George Fox, who founded the Society of Quakers in the seventeenth century. He knew other books from the period as well, which was the most animated period of English history, and from when many of the most important religious movements dated. It was not an educated conversation, for that I had—unfortunately—Mr Milburn. The street sweeper was about eighty, but seemed as hale as a man of fifty. Intellectually, he was even younger than that, in the way he asked his questions, which he would go on doing to the end of his life. He never spoke for too long, and he had a way of stopping abruptly, as though to think something through, before resuming the conversation. On the next occasion, he never pedantically picked up the thread where we had left it, but he showed me that he had remembered all of it, down to the smallest details. There was nothing redundant in these conversations. Nor was there anything formulaic, as in most conversations in our day. One indication of that is that he never once talked about the weather, even though there was occasion enough to do so. Once, I saw him standing hesitating in a rain shower, and I felt too bashful to offer him, he who was so much older than I was, my umbrella, and when I had finally plucked up courage to do so, and went up to him, he just stood under it. Even in the rain, he refused to waste a word on it.

In the course of those years, I met many of the local people. He was the only one whom I wholeheartedly loved. One day, when we had learned of the most terrible things, in incontrovertible details, he took two steps up to me, which he had never yet done, and said: "I'm sorry for what's happening to your people." And then he added: "They are my people too."

(He lived alone in a hut nearby. He was never ill. One time, when he failed to turn out for two days in a row, I knew what had happened. There are only four or five people in my life whom I mourned as I mourned him.)

HERBERT READ

He belonged to those poets who were formed by the First World War, in particular the trench warfare in Northern France. Two of them died young: Wilfred Owen and Isaac Rosenberg. Two more remained alive, and lived to a great age: Siegfried Sassoon and Herbert Read. He was the one I knew. I do not want to write about our first meeting now, which was over lunch with a third person before the beginning of the Second World War, the third person became a friend to me, and I saw him every week over several years. He deserves a chapter to himself, when I get to him.

The second time I met Herbert Read, then, the War had already begun. We were by then living in Chesham Bois, and a librarian at the Victoria and Albert Museum, who had moved into a house on the same street as ours, was giving a party for artists, scholars and arts people, to which we had been invited. This was one of those crowded, stand-up parties that are so characteristic of England, which I could never get used to, and even now, after fifty years, find myself bemused by. The atmosphere in this instance was a little more cordial than it sometimes is, a lot of people had been evacuated on account of the air war, and were living in the Chilterns as we were, others had taken the train out from London after work, just to be there, and perhaps it was this combination of exceptional circumstances that made for a more congenial atmosphere. I didn't know anyone there, beyond the master of the house and his wife, all the other faces were new to me. There were painters present, who were pursuing a new type of painting, produced by the new predicaments of the air war, honestly and often compellingly responding to this wholly new experience. I recognised them among the many other guests, they stood out, some by their sharply etched facial features, others by their unexpectedly withdrawn manner. I tried to understand some of these latter. Their appearance was so much at variance with their sudden celebrity, that I was overcome by astonishment and awe. I was trying to cope with it, as they did with their fame, discreetly, almost like a pupil, when I saw someone whose face seemed familiar to me, I must have seen him before, but I couldn't remember where, and didn't know who he was. He was a master of discretion, he outdid everyone else in this, not just my own pitiable beginner's efforts. To all the others, he seemed almost not to be there at all. If my thoughts had not been compelled in his direction, I should never have made the attempt to compare one of these recessives with another, and I'm sure I would never even have noticed him. It wasn't some external form of behaviour that he had worked to acquire, it was expressive of his nature. Something in his bearing was suggestive of a soldier. But there was nothing boastful about it, he was a disappointed soldier, which was what he remained, because he was never able to put his experience and his disappointment behind him. He wasn't by any means mute, he was involved in a conversation that soon broke off, whereupon he turned to someone else, who asked him a question. I tried to move nearer to him, in the hope of recognising him, but since he couldn't get away, this was a tricky undertaking. Finally, I was so close to him that he could not help but notice me, he recognised me, smiled, and—in a way that seemed distinctly warmer—he spoke my name. This was

Herbert Read. I remembered him in the instant he said my name, because that look of solid friendliness was the one with which he had looked at me as we sat over lunch, the three of us.

He asked me whether I was living here. He was just as surprised to see me as I was to see him. No-one had thought to tell me he was expected. No-one knew we were acquainted. Perhaps the key to these bewildering English gatherings is meeting (and recognising) someone one has seen once before, and then not for a long time. Later too, when we knew one another better, there was always something shy about him. I think it was important to him not to issue any commands. He was, I knew, the head of a respected publishing house, took his work very seriously, and wrote books on modern art that were widely read. I do not know if he was still writing poems, or prose, like that fine story of early life that made his name: *The Innocent Eye*.

So there he was, this clever, withdrawn man, talking to painters about their art. Each of them tried to arouse his interest, and yet he remained marked by his true experience, which was that of the disappointed soldier. Because we met at a time that he abominated. He could not get over the fact that it was war again, not the trench war he had been through, but a dynamic modern war, with armour and air power. Paris had already fallen, it was the year of British isolation. The war with Russia had not yet begun. I was certain it would come, and told him, too, perhaps partly to comfort him, because he asked me what I thought about England's solitary resistance, and whether I thought it had any chance of success. What most profoundly concerned him was not that England might lose the War, so much as the fact that there was war at all—he didn't say this to me, but I ventured to intuit it. He was a little taken aback by the certainty with which I was expecting the attack on

Russia. From our first meeting, two years before, he remembered what I was working on, and asked me whether it was my thinking about crowds that had led me to this conclusion. I told him it was not, but that I also thought a lot about the history of those in power, and I therefore was in no doubt that Hitler's deepest desire was to outdo Napoleon. He didn't disagree, but he gently shook his head. That's how I see him now, when I think about him, doubting and yet engaged. Many years later, the War long past, this engagement of his was to be beneficial to my work.

VICES AND VIRTUES
OF ENGLISH PARTIES

One could write a book about English parties. I never got used to them. They strike me as senseless and heartless, every bit in keeping with such cold people. The idea, after all, is not to get too close. As soon as a conversation was developing (which wasn't an easy thing to bring about), it was time to push off and turn to somebody else. It was not done to spend too long with one person, that was accounted selfish. People were there to make rapid contact, and, still more, rapid withdrawals. Sometimes you wouldn't even know who you had been talking to. Those were the ideal cases in these ritualised celebrations of non-contact.

There may be people who think of English conviviality as exemplary, as a spur to tolerance and universal respect. I am not of their number, and have never felt unhappier than when taking up these invitations. Part of the point was having a lot of people in a limited space, it was almost to be a crush, and yet they were supposed to take avoiding action, and not so much as brush against one another. The art of them is standing terribly close to someone else, and betraying nothing significant of oneself. And not to let on. You are one among many. Whoever is anything out of the ordinary must diligently conceal the fact.

The summit of the art is not vouchsafing one's name. When introduced, you mumble it as unclearly as possible. That only adds to the weight of the significant name, which the other does secretly sense. Whoever comes from nowhere, i.e. nowhere in England, doesn't exist, and for that, he is treated with even more politeness, the more exquisite the less he is perceived to matter.

I am not talking here about gatherings of university people. Such people have a professional claim to curiosity, or, at the very least, to a show of curiosity about the other's specialism. Someone who is capable of going from specialist to specialist, and listening to each speaking in his own way, can only become a writer, and is bound to achieve regard.

But these Oxford and Cambridge instances, which can actually be quite interesting, are a special case, and not what I am talking about.

The pre-condition of the English party is that people are distributed among various castes, and occasionally admit into their midst other people of different castes, to provide a little variety. Never will anyone who comes from a lower caste be made to feel this. So long as he does not draw any inappropriate conclusions from the fact that he has been invited to a party. He should not drop names, and people he has been able to meet in this way are to be protected from any subsequent contact with him.

It is permissible to ask cautious questions, so long as one avoids being indiscreet. One may not ask too long or insistently. Behind that is a correct understanding of what a question is, namely a means to power. People who, asked, go into too much detail about their line of work are categorised as foreigners, and are socially contemptible, even though they may be deserving in all kinds of ways.

HAMPSTEAD:
AT A GATHERING OF POETS

In the winter of '44–5, the last of the War, Paris had been liberated, Pierre Emmanuel, a French poet, active in the Resistance, came to London. Some English poets gave a party for him. They assembled in William Empson's "basement", and each of them read a poem in Emmanuel's honour, or sometimes two.

There were many there whom I had never seen, including—in accordance with the polite but implacably hierarchic laws of English society—Eliot himself. Dylan Thomas was there, and so were many others, so many that I can't remember them all, only those of them I got to know better later on. Friedl, who had published two books in 1944, took me along. I was a total unknown to the English, among these twenty or thirty poets I was a *nobody*, I had lived in their country for five years, but had published nothing. I was there as a friend and tutor of Friedl's, someone to whom she had dedicated both her novels. Empson's wife, Hetta, a close friend of Friedl's and a very handsome woman who looked like a Renoir, spoke German, and had heard me reading my piece, "The Good Father". She received me with honour, singling me out; where there was some particularly fine bottle, she said: "Reserved for you and Mr Eliot." That did me good, and I did not feel too humiliated, even though—apart from Friedl—she was the only person there who knew anything about me.

This is where I first met Kathleen Raine, who was a modest, dignified presence in this gathering. She read out of a large, lined, hardbound notebook. I spoke to her afterwards, I liked the simplicity of her notebook, and she showed it to me quite unfussily. There was a pleasing *naturel*, and, as I say, modesty, to her. It did not seem to matter to her that she didn't know the first thing about me. I had no idea at the time of the arrogance there was concealed behind such modesty. Arrogance is such an integral part of the English, one often fails to notice it. They take arrogance to new, unsuspected levels.

The best instance of that was Eliot. There he sat, the terribly famous man among all those others, amidst whom there were certainly many bad poets whom he must despise from the depths of his being, and he gave no indication of the fact, at least not in the distance he kept from the others. It was a bare basement room, quite a large space, and he sat in the midst of all these people, there was hardly room for him to stretch out his arms without bumping into someone else. But he seemed not to feel constricted, or at least not to show it if he did. His features were impassive, there was very little movement in them. The puritanical aspect of the occasion must have been something he was familiar with from his youth, and the stoical side he had probably acquired in the course of his time in England. Still, he certainly received privileged treatment. Because, after he had read a poem, the dark, gold-tooth-flashing figure of Pierre Emmanuel asked him to read it a second time. One could tell how closely he was attending, his mouth was half open, he weighed every word on the gold scales of his teeth, before letting it pass satisfied to his ears. In this, he was supported by the pushy Sonia Brownell, whose Rubenesque upper body was draped in a dazzling white silk blouse. "Would Mr Eliot read another poem?" Eliot obeyed, without haste, without eagerness, as calmly as though he was oblivious to the request. If anything, he seemed even a little surprised to be asked for more.

But I don't want to talk about Eliot now, though there would be quite a bit to say on his influence at that time. I return to Kathleen Raine, whom I first met at this honorious convocation of English poets. She had a natural self-confidence, answered any question calmly and unpompously, was happy to let me look at her notebook, where there was a lot written, and not just poems. I felt well around her, among all these people who didn't know me, and who didn't have the least desire to know me. She invited me to call on her. I think she already knew Friedl. She was a close friend of Sonia Brownell, who had an influential job on Cyril Connolly's magazine, *Horizon*.

Dylan Thomas read, in his singing, florid manner, the diametrical opposite to Eliot's barren dryness. He had become famous during the War, a very young man with a cherub's face, everyone talked about him, who had nothing but nothing in common with Eliot. Of course, he too was asked for an encore by Emmanuel. His language, nourished by Shakespeare as much as by his Welsh roots, wasn't easy to understand in its concentrated rhetoric. But Emmanuel's gold teeth did not betray that they flashed in vain. Even so, his mouth hung a little further open, showing a black gullet full of miasmas. The contrast between Eliot and Dylan Thomas, who sat not far apart, could hardly have been greater. But jammed in as they were among so many others, it lost its edge, and seemed almost historical. In the historical dimension, there is room for all sorts of things, there is so much and more all the time, and its variousness makes it seem to belong, otherwise it wouldn't be remarked. A little surprising is the fact that there was a historian there as well, of whom the clueless assembly remained unaware, a historian not of the usual sort, but a descendant of Aubrey.

A critic by the name of Scott sat next to Friedl and me, stern, inflexible of face. After Dylan Thomas had read his long poem twice over, he remarked: "He's like Swinburne." Today I understand what he meant, but at the time it seemed to me to have been said critically, and since I was passionately in favour of anything that promised to relieve Eliot's authority, I irritated him with an icy response to his remark.

I won't go into the many other things that happened that evening. They do not seem so important to me now, because they didn't have any personal consequences for me. All I really intended was to recollect where and how I first met Kathleen Raine, in whose life I was to play an important role. She, meanwhile, was significant in the external framing of mine.

KATHLEEN RAINE

I often went to her parties in Chelsea. For many years I was a constant guest of hers. Often I went with Friedl, at a time when she was already passionately rebelling against me, but even then she got herself noticed as my companion. There were men who only noticed me because they were envious. Decades later, I would run into men who asked after her. One of them was the sculptor Paolozzi.

My early acquaintance with Kathleen Raine was confined to a few, infrequent invitations. Over a few years, while I was still in the company of Friedl, the acquaintance failed to deepen. This changed later, when Clement Glock introduced me to the Maxwell brothers, Gavin and Aymer. They weren't twins, but they were fraternal enemies. Their rivalry determined their lives. Their mother was a daughter of the Duke of Northumberland, they were Percys, though no longer pure-blooded. Percys appear in Shakespeare, which made the name doubly significant for Kathleen.

Among the people I knew for many years without ever really liking, is the poet Kathleen Raine. I always listened to her; each time she told me her tear-bedewed story, I listened. I don't know where I got the patience from. Her complaints were invariably boring. I knew that not a word of it was true, all of it was illusory, and the persistence of the illusion was such that I would sometimes disbelievingly remind myself: well, she is a poet after all. But she doesn't know when. She is when she grieves for a fantasy, a single true love—would to God there had been more of them. She had spent her childhood in Northumberland. Her father was a schoolmaster, descended from Methodist coal miners, who went down into the ground singing hymns, and after long, back-breaking toil, were hoisted back up to the surface, singing all the way. Her mother was Scottish, of higher birth, perhaps, as Kathleen hoped, she was even from the Highlands, and she told arrogant and eerie stories. There had been wars between the English and the Scots over hundreds of years. One of the bravest knights on the English side was Percy Hotspur, who is celebrated in *Henry IV*, he was the ancestor of those Dukes of Northumberland who had their seat at Alnwick Castle.

When they were out walking once, Kathleen's mother pointed out to her a couple of golden, shining-haired boys who were standing together on a small bridge. Their mother was speaking to them in elevated tones, the language was like poetry. This was Lady Mary, the daughter of the Duke, with her boys, who, if not the *sons* of a Duke, were at least grandsons.

The vision of the two golden-haired boys was to accompany Kathleen all her life. Thirty years later, when I knew her, she still spoke about it in visionary terms. She had studied at Cambridge, is said to have been a beauty, was admired by some of the students, and published poems that impressed poets like Edwin Muir and Herbert Read. She had forsaken the embarrassing Methodism of her father, and converted to Catholicism, had been a Buddhist for a while, engrossing herself in its sects, reverted to Catholicism, and wound up a Jungian. There she felt well, visibly, there I think she had the sense of getting all religions at once, didn't need to give any one up for another . . . now with one, now with another, and finally for her life's work on William Blake (her favourite among the English poets) in all seriousness cited Jung as evidence. It was—this may sound harsh—like using some modern contraption like a computer to explain the Bible. I knew her for many years, and we had lengthy conversations, in which we kept returning to religion. Try as I might to object to Jung's banalities, she retained her expression of faintly ironic superiority, because in Jung she thought she had a universal key, one that fitted anywhere. She never despised me, though; for her I was an Old Testament character—for *her*, I say, lest anyone misunderstand—and the fierce passion of some of the prophets had—for Scottish reasons, as it were—a hold on her. It was all battles and victories, vengeance was exacted, there was no forgiveness, peoples were exterminated at the decrees of the Almighty, how much good that did her after all the dutiful lip service to mercy and compassion was something I only gradually realised.

I think her friendship, which to her was a perfectly genuine friendship, was sustained by her notion of the primal vehemence of my belief, and even though I did not have any such thing, she had a completely mistaken view of me. Not for a moment did she see me as a writer, the little she was able to read of mine struck her as tasteless, though she was careful never to tell me so. I, however, always knew it, and thought with some satisfaction how little *her* poems did for *me*. In some way, then, it was a false friendship. It is strange to realise this, when I think how much gravity, concern and endeavour I expended over many years trying to help her with the difficulties of her life.

The religious conversations to which she was forever returning, her unshakeable reverence for Jung as the key to every religion, masked some far more profound thing in her, for which she fought tooth and claw: the attaining of the two golden-haired boys, or at least one of them. The two grandsons of the Duke, whom one might have thought to be twins but actually weren't, were born eighteen months apart, and that was of great importance to the composition of her life. The elder of the two, Aymer, was heir to a great estate, a castle with extensive acres in Galloway, the southernmost county in Scotland. He was heir to the title as well. He was only a baronet, but it was a very old baronetcy, I think going back to the Normans. His mother, Lady Mary, as already mentioned, was the daughter of the Duke of Northumberland, and thereby more or less a Percy. That was the only thing that really mattered to Kathleen, and I am quite convinced that the two brothers, gold lustre and all, didn't remind her at all of their mother. Gavin, the younger, was fobbed off, as happens in these cases, with a sum of money that he spent in little or no time. Following his Percy uncle, the brother of his mother, he had studied zoology. As happens in such circles, he had become a splendid shot and hunter. His boldness and his eye were both equally good. When he suddenly found himself in possession of his limited inheritance, he decided to buy a small island south of Skye, and set up a little factory to process shark. He became a renowned shark fisherman, and did considerable damage among the species. Even so, the enterprise refused to flourish, and he ended up having to sell the island, I think it was Kathleen whom he met at about this time, who advised him to write about his experiences as a shark fisherman, and that was how his first book came to be written. *Harpoon at a Venture* it was called, and it was a great success. His introduction to the world of books, and everything that flowed from that, he owed to Kathleen. She was indefatigable, she introduced him to every single person who might be useful to him, she gave parties for him in her Chelsea house. He had the bold features of a mariner, a somewhat weathered Viking. His dangerous pursuits had left their traces, the golden hair was already a memory. He had a profound love of animals, even in London he always had one or two. From later expeditions, he would bring some back with him. In the swamps of southern Iraq, he discovered a new type of otter which was named after him, and he brought a cub back to London with him, and raised it there, Mysbel was its name.

The two brothers soon got into the habit of visiting me, to talk about themselves and their struggles with each other. They could spend hours on the subject, they never tired of it, and I listened to them with honest fascination.

AYMER AND HIS MOTHER

ere I interrupt the story of Gavin, which always
becomes insufferably boring where it touches that of
Kathleen, and turn to his elder brother, Aymer, who
became a very good friend of mine. After the early death of his
father, who fell at the very beginning of the First World War,
a young Captain, the two brothers grew up with their mother,
Lady Mary, and two younger siblings in a modest house not far
from the family pile at Monreith. In Monreith lived the
grandfather of the two, Sir Herbert Maxwell, probably the
most respected man in Galloway. For many years, he
discharged all the public duties that came his way, without
overweening, to the universal satisfaction. He was an
outstanding breeder of trees and flowers; the rhododendron
woods at Monreith are internationally famous. He studied
Celtic languages, and engaged in antiquarian studies on the
early history of Scotland. He wrote numerous books on his
various special fields—I didn't know many of them—in the
clear, readable, and yet far from superficial manner of the
Victorians. Whether he had the humour and sense of mockery
of his grandsons, I am not able to say, I never knew him. He
grew very old, if I can believe Aymer's account, past ninety. At
the time I got to know Aymer, he had inherited from him. His
grandfather, for whose death Aymer had waited impatiently,
had died just a little earlier. Aymer shared none of the interests

of his venerable forefather. He had a stammer—I always thought it was from impatience, he was one of the quickest and busiest people I ever met.

Their mother, Lady Mary, had raised both boys in the serious, fundamentalist faith of the Catholic Apostolic Church. The founder of this faith, Edward Irving, one of the great preachers of the early nineteenth century, was a close friend of Carlyle, and is described in some detail and unforgettably in his autobiography. He came out of the Presbyterian Church, which was the dominant church in Scotland, and founded the Catholic Apostolic Church as a dissenting sect. It took root among all levels of the population, including—and this was a little unusual for a movement of this type—the high aristocracy. The Dukes of Northumberland were among its adherents. This led to the building of large and imposing churches, in London alone there must be half a dozen of them. But, since no other ducal families joined that creed, it meant that a daughter of the Percys was rather limited in terms of the choice of possible bridegrooms. Lady Mary married a son of Sir Herbert Maxwell. The Maxwells had also joined this church.

Lady Mary was serious about her Christianity (so much so that her only daughter, Christine, Aymer's sister, later became a Communist), but, for all the humility she brought to her faith, she remained moulded by her origins: she had a proud, handsome face, spoke in clear, cut-glass tones that showed, even when she was very old, that she was used to giving commands, quite without arrogance. She met Veza as if on equal terms, took a perfectly genuine interest in everything she said, *accepted* her as a writer, which not many did in those days, and talked to her about Dante and Petrarch, whom she had read in Florence, as a girl.

VISIT IN MOCHRUM

Aymer was wonderfully entertaining, and told the most amusing stories about his neighbours, landowners like himself, who lived some distance away and whom he called on, as was the custom, from time to time. There was one whom he especially wanted to show me, an eccentric of a kind one only ever finds in Scotland: Lord David Stewart, a scion of the Bute family. He lived at Mochrum, a mediaeval castle with thick walls, alone with his wife Ursula. He was a passionate birdwatcher, who would often take off for weeks at a time,

Elias Canetti in Scotland, 1951

looking for some rare breed, and he knew the remotest islands and shores of Scotland.

He also had a serious lung condition, which sometimes kept him bedridden, and then he would receive us in pyjamas and dressing-gown. There he lay, a lean man with a dark, sharply etched face and a suspicious expression on it. When we were introduced, his eyes took me in contemptuously, I only saw later that he was short, when he got up to show us round one of the remote islands that belonged to him. He spoke very little, and still less when he was lying in bed. Aymer asked how he was, and he only said: "Bad. Bad." But, as I found out later, he wasn't feeling any worse than usual, he just had to say something disparaging about himself. He was known for his habitual pessimism, he expected the worst of everyone, and for that reason lived alone with his wife, of whose social inclinations he took no notice. She ordered the newest fashions from Paris, and wore them—well, for whom? Certainly not for her husband, who wasn't in the least bit interested. But nor for anyone else either, because the handful of neighbours, who all lived some way off, rarely came, as he was always rude to them. One of the very few who were occasionally admitted was Aymer. Aymer's tone in his conversations with Lady Ursula, who was fading away in her beauty, had something plaintive about it. I was puzzled, with me he was always exuberant, and his poisonous and hilarious accounts of people had him stammering in no time. With Lady Ursula, he spoke slowly, never said much, and ended with some wistful and sympathetic lament. Lord David asked his wife to show us round the castle. That was the object of our visit, Aymer knew it well enough already, of course, he had announced our visit by telephone, and emphasised how much his friend, a writer, was looking forward to seeing the castle. That he had said something else as well, I learned only later. Lady Ursula was only too happy to take us round. We went through narrow passages that seemed unending, the castle with its thick walls—it was built in the fifteenth century—was positively labyrinthine. One could easily wander around it for ever, not noticing that it was often in the same passages. Lady Ursula was in one of her Parisian numbers, which would have excited interest and admiration had she been among people, here it was just a case of craning round the gloomy passages, but once, as we came to a corner, I seemed to notice how her trailing silken sleeves lightly brushed against Aymer. He did not notice it himself, but it must have been important to her, because when we returned to the room where her husband lay bedridden, her face was lit by something that all three of us noticed. The effect on her husband was remarkable. He asked whether I had a good *eye*. Before I could think what to say by way of reply, he said roughly to his wife: "Bring me the yellow stone!" She went, and a while later returned, and handed him a ring with a very large yellow diamond in it. "What d'you think it's worth?" I was bewildered, I didn't know what to say, luckily I guessed straightaway what must have happened. Aymer must have told him on the telephone that the man coming to visit him was a Jew. Aymer himself wasn't in the least prejudiced. No-one I met in England ever showed me any anti-Semitic feeling. If there had ever been any, then Einstein and Freud had done their bit. It's hard to do justice to the fame of those two in the Anglo-Saxon world. They are cultural heroes, benefactors of mankind. But Aymer, who was incredibly tactful, must have known how boorish Lord David could be. Perhaps he had once heard him talk of a jeweller, and that would have been the only Jew of his acquaintance. To save me from possible embarrassment, he would have told his neighbour of the origin of the writer who was coming to visit him. He thought that doing so would obviate any trifling irritation for me, and him as well, but precisely the opposite occurred. The attractiveness of his wife put Lord David in mind of the stone he had recently given her. He thought it was a useful opportunity to find out whether he had bought prudently, and so he asked me to value the stone. I felt so offended that I gave him an answer: "Fifty thousand." It was meant to sound just as abrupt, foolish and imperious as his question. "That's exactly what I paid for it," he said. "Good. They didn't cheat me."

When a profusely apologetic Aymer asked me later how I had happened to hit on this figure, he refused to believe I wanted simply to *avenge* myself. It was meant to sound random and outrageous, and to *shame* the master of the house. We talked about it, and finally agreed that it must be telepathy. Was there any gift that my friend would not have attributed to me?

The owner, or rather, the giver, of this enormous yellow diamond complained that his wife would never wear the ring.

On the monastery island at Mochrum, 1950

"She's too modest," he said. "Or she has too much taste," said Aymer, and for that she flashed him a touchingly winning smile, for which I envied him.

Finally, the lord of the house got up, and suggested we visit a monastery island that was some half an hour away. Aymer had never been there, and we agreed. The drive to the loch where the island was situated seemed pleasingly long to me. On the shore was a boat, and we rowed out and found the ruin of a Celtic monastery on an island. I asked Lord David who owned the ruin. "It's mine!" he said, so emphatically, as if it had not been the island, but the whole planet. On another island, not far away, there were innumerable cormorants. It was the furthest distance from the sea anywhere in Scotland that had a brood of cormorants. That island, the loch, and the whole stretch of land we'd driven over, all of it belonged to him. A visit there he would not countenance, on account of the terrible smell. Perhaps it was that cormorant island, which he had known all his life, that had made him an ornithologist.

LORD DAVID STEWART

Lord David did not seem at all put out by the noise the cormorants were making. We could at least hear ourselves speaking on the monastery island. I had the sense the island had never been properly explored. But that couldn't be the case. The interest in the past in Scotland, of any period, was far too developed for that to be possible. It was the way Lord David had of separating his property from the rest of the world that gave me such an impression.

More than anything else, he needed silence. It was difficult to find servants for Mochrum who were sufficiently self-effacing. For a while he kept a Polish couple, the man as butler, his wife as housekeeper. A lot of soldiers of the Polish army had stayed behind in Scotland after the War. They were well liked, and since they could not go home, they settled in the country. The ex-colonel whom Lord David took on had perfect manners, as he reluctantly admitted, but he also had a loud laugh. His wife on occasion would laugh with him. As a couple they were entirely satisfactory, only they laughed too readily, and too often. It made life intolerable for the laird in his gloomy halls. So he dismissed them, and for a while he had no-one at all.

He was often away from home, looking for rare birds. He was particularly smitten with the sea coasts. He liked visiting lighthouses, and sought out those with single occupants. There, he would even enter conversation, because everyone knew who he was, answered respectfully to his questions, and, above all, never said more than he wanted to know. On one occasion, he was surprised to find, in a lighthouse in the remote north, a young man who felt thoroughly at home in his solitude, who didn't even need to insist on the fact to him. He was asked how he bore it. "Very easily," came the reply. How long had he been there already?—Two years—How would he like to come south, to be a butler at his castle? The young man, overwhelmed at having been engaged in personal conversation with Lord David, quickly agreed.

He came, and Lord David liked him, and Lord David's wife liked him. He never laughed, or not so that one was aware of it. Nor was he moody either, he was bright and punctual, and he followed every instruction without ever asking for a reason. He understood his master's every wish, even before he had spoken them. Generally, a word or two would suffice, there wasn't even the need for a whole sentence. His nature was so ideal that he once—briefly—even told Aymer about him, who had difficulties of his own with staff, and was astonished at his neighbour's good fortune.

Lady Ursula never wore the dresses she ordered from Paris more than once, not in public at least. What she did when she was alone, no-one could say. Nor was there anyone there who would have been interested (would have racked their brains on the subject). She knew very well though what dresses she had, and it bothered her when she found herself looking for one, and was unable to find it. It happened again, and then again, over many months and years. She did not say anything to her husband, but she pondered the matter. One day—the dress that had disappeared had been particularly beautiful, when he'd been shown it, her husband had gone so far as to nod his head approvingly—she turned up without warning in the remote room of the young man. She found the way, which she had never gone before (and which was quite a distance in this castle), stood in front of the door, and suddenly pushed it open, to find herself confronting the young man, wearing the missing dress, standing in front of a mirror enraptured, and striking a few balletic poses.

He felt discovered, but not caught, greeted his mistress with a few dignified sentences, and told her that, more than anything, he loved the ballet, and had only taken the job here in the south of Scotland, because it was halfway to London. That was his true destination, the ballet there, and now he would set off. He had tried on all of her dresses and put them all back, only two or three that fitted him particularly well, he had been reluctant to return, and kept putting off the moment. There was so much praise for her dresses that she set aside some of it for herself. He was as loquacious as someone in a Shakespeare play. Where had he learned to talk like that? She would never have said such things, but she was as helpless before them, as if they had been said to her. She did not seem to herself to have been robbed (just imagine it, in Scotland, or anywhere else in the world), she took it as a tribute to her taste, and perhaps—though she would never have admitted this—for more than that. In the most charming way, he now gave back the remaining dresses in his possession, there were three in all. The two that he wasn't wearing he returned immediately, and, in politely lofty words, he asked her kindly to leave him on his own, so that he might now take off the third.

She went back the long way alone, and for the next hour or so, avoided her own rooms. When she could no longer stand it, and finally went there, she found all three dresses neatly in place. No-one could have told that they had ever been worn. It was as though they had just arrived from Paris, he could not even tell from looking at them that she had worn them once for her husband.

The young lighthouse keeper went straight to her husband, and asked to be allowed to leave. He needed to go to London right away, and asked his employer to waive his period of notice. Lord David said: "But you haven't had any sudden news, has your father died?" He knew what came in the post, and he knew the young man had never received a single letter in all his time there. He could not discuss it, said the other, he had simply to leave right away. Lord David was rather annoyed,

Aymer Maxwell

but on the other hand he was grateful that he pressed no claims of any sort, and did not even want his back pay. He was also relieved, because the young man turned out not to be so taciturn, he was suddenly speaking like someone unafraid of loquacity, and with his every sentence provoked such repugnance in his master that he was pleased to be shot of him. He left in that same hour, without taking leave of his lady. When Lord David told his wife, "He's gone," not more than that, she nodded in satisfaction. He had not even known that she had disliked the young man. He was happy, though, because she had never talked to him about it.

For her part, she was relieved that she had not mentioned the vanishing of her dresses. She told him nothing. The next time Aymer came, she asked him out for a walk, and told him the whole story. She had to tell someone. But it took a lot of words to explain the whole episode. She didn't think her husband would be willing to listen to such a long account. More likely, he would be irritated by so much talk. To charge the young man with theft made no sense either. Everything had been returned, and she did not want to become the subject of gossip. Aymer told her she had done well. He would tell her husband some time, ideally when they were out shooting together.

And so it was left, not a word was exchanged about the matter between husband and wife. Who the next butler at Mochrum was, I never learned.

MRS PHILLIMORE
BERTRAND RUSSELL

There is so much to say about Mrs Phillimore that I hardly know where to begin. She was a very old lady, and kept a suite high up in the Ritz. She was big and raw-boned, and received her guests in a colourful oriental fantasia of brocade. One had the sense that she was exquisitely dressed, but it wasn't to make any impression with her wealth. Because she had always been wealthy, at least since the time of her marriage, it was an old English jurisprudential family she had married into, with property in Ireland, where she had lived in one of the big houses for a time. Her husband had died early, she never talked about him, he had made no impression on her, for more than fifty years she had lived alone. When she moved from Ireland to a large estate north of London, she became a neighbour to George Bernard Shaw, whom she saw very often, and with whom she loved to converse. She was quick-witted, *maline*, and just as tireless as he. It appears that he liked her society as well, because when he was away, he wrote her letters, all of which she kept. She occasionally showed off her great bundle of Shaw letters, without ever letting anyone read them. She measured the intellect of the innumerable people she saw against Shaw's; it is no wonder that most of them bored her.

In the War, she was already fairly old when the British government found a useful job for her. She was made a sort of semi-official hostess in London, and was called upon to entertain all the foreign governments who were in exile in England. Before long, she knew exactly where she was, and found the right tone for every minister and ambassador. It's hard to imagine the number of governments that at that time found themselves in London, courtesy of the British government. She knew them all, even the most stubborn among them, the ones who didn't make anything easy for the English, and set her own nationalistically-tinged pride against theirs. The man she mentioned most often in her accounts was the most difficult of all, namely de Gaulle. With all her mockery, she would never have dared to claim that he had ever engaged in conversation with her. He was so abrupt and impossible to influence that she developed a secret, never admitted *faible* for him, even though he was opposed to all things Anglo-Saxon. Her true yardstick, though, remained Shaw, and what foreign minister was there who could compete with him in witty formulations and surprises?

She had written a book, but not set her name to it, and yet this book was one of the biggest sellers of the time. With the royalties from it, she might, as she said a little playfully, have paid for the suite at the Ritz and the dinner parties herself. The book was called, *He*, and it was by an "Unknown Disciple". Of course the unknown disciple was herself, and "He" was Jesus. I never read it, she wrote at some time at the beginning of the century. Its success was perfectly predictable in the English-language territory. I don't think the book as such went to her head. But she was always aware of the trappings of success, and she despised authors who didn't sell. The contradiction between the subject of the book, and her sales-consciousness never struck her. But from it she derived her claim to deal with any author as an equal, and, when she factored in her dealings with Shaw, she soon went on to claim superiority.

She had deep black piercing eyes in a narrow high face, with a jutting brow that seemed almost unhealthily high. Everything about her was black, and maybe it was just her malice that gave one the sense that her eyes were piercing. For all her liveliness, she might have been a hundred, and perhaps she wasn't much less than that in actuality. Politically, she would have inclined towards the Fabians, without being at all irritating. She wasn't a creature of system, and she does not seem to have sought out the Webbs. As I say, in everything that appertained to this world, her thing was Shaw. But she was—and had been, I suspected, for quite some time—more imbued by the other world, for which she did sterling work. If she came across someone who was not of the faith, she would at the very least try to recruit him for the "Society for Psychic Research", for which she was an organiser. She believed firmly in ghosts, and had amassed a personal tally of at least a hundred "supernatural encounters".

If one continued to express reservations, she would resort to threats. On more than one occasion, she levelled her eyes at me like daggers, and said: "I shall come back and haunt you!" She looked forward to all the evil doings that lay open to her after her death, and perhaps that was the main reason why she insisted, with almost fiendish adamancy, that the soul was immortal.

She had moved into the Ritz a long time ago, and to begin with things had not looked good for her there. In the top-floor suite where she lived, she felt miserable at first, crushed and pursued, and did not understand why, until she learned that her bedroom had seen a notorious suicide. A man from a respected family, the son of an admiral, I believe, had leapt out of the window, and lay in Piccadilly with a shattered skull. It wasn't all that long ago, and she might have felt apprehension about moving into the Ritz at all, had the atmosphere there not been so familiar to her from many parties she had given there during the War. She had had no idea though, about the suite she had been given. She was the first guest to stay in the unhappy man's bedroom since, and for her that was the ultimate proof that her convictions were justified, that what she had been feeling for weeks had been the unhappiness of the soul that inhabited the place. Finally, a waiter had taken pity on her, and told her the secret of the place. She straightaway had some priests come from Brompton Oratory, and exorcise the unhappy spirit for her.

She changed her suite nevertheless, and told every one of her new guests, at a first visit, what had happened in the hotel. That made it easy to get back to her favourite topic, even after I'd known her for a year, she would keep talking about her experiences with ghosts. The most convincing—for her the most irrefutable—was the one with the suicide in the Ritz.

Years before, she had rented one of the houses on my friend Aymer's estate in Galloway. There she had spent the six summer months, and occasionally met Aymer. He was about fifty years her junior, and barely noticed her. He had come into his inheritance from his grandfather, who was a great expert in many different things, in the languages and history of the Celts, in horticulture and dendriculture—one of the great rhododendron breeders of the time, he had planted whole forests of them on his land—who had written a number of books of the sort that find a grateful public in the British Isles. One cannot really dismiss them as popular science, because they are full of inferences drawn, basically, from their author's personal experience. His son and heir had been one of the first men to die in the Great War. Aymer, the grandson, had had to wait a long time for his grandfather, a man full of knowledge and wisdom, the most respected in the community, to pass on. Then the time finally came, and the young baronet came into his inheritance. He was unlike his grandfather in all respects, witty, vivacious, mostly on his travels, with no interest in dry knowledge, and much too restless to content himself with the day-to-day management of a large estate. It was from him that Mrs Phillimore had rented one of the more remote properties on the estate, not too close to the main house, which he himself occupied. He was bold, swift and resolute, an outstanding shot, still very fond of going out shooting. He appeared more bloodthirsty than actually he was, at first blush he seemed every inch a Viking. One couldn't but associate him with the most risky adventures, even though he hadn't experienced any. Also, when he was in society, he was often afflicted with a bad stammer, which seemed quite at variance with his appearance. Nonetheless, Mrs Phillimore became obsessed with him. She had known innumerable people in her life, among them some utterly eccentric and exceptional types, and yet it was with him and him alone that she was obsessed. It did not greatly concern him, women did not interest him, as a good and sought-after match, he tended to be wary of them, and only had dealings with them if they were in firm hands, and hence not a potential danger to him. He needed have no fear of old Mrs Phillimore. When he moved down to London, where he soon became my friend, he would accept occasional dinner invitations from her. She knew she could only lure him to her by dangling exceptionally interesting, famous or strange personalities as a bait. To me he had told everything about himself, he liked me, and I liked him as an apparently fiery, wild, but in fact utterly inscrutable character. He told me of many dinner invitations he had received from Mrs Phillimore, admitted that she had succeeded in tempting him by letting him know who else was expected, but still he never went, because he felt too abashed by his own ignorance. At the back of his mind always was his omniscient grandfather, who had oppressed and alarmed him by the sheer volume of what he knew. He would implore me to get to know the old devil, as he persisted in referring to Mrs Phillimore. He was certain she would make an impression on me, with my predilection for strange and scurrilous characters. I could still always decide for myself whether or not I wanted to go, and if I did, then he would be happy to go along himself, he was very curious about some of her guests, but he needed the company of a friend to protect him in his own ignorance.

I soon gave in to his pleas, and never regretted it. Already at the very first dinner of hers that I attended, she spoke about ghosts, Bernard Shaw and Bertrand Russell, all in one lump. The last of these she had known well in his early years, she had been the closest friend of his first wife, Alice. She kept talking about Bertie, and it took us a little while to realise who she was referring to. There wasn't a trace of respect for him in the way she talked, whereas I was full of admiration for his current position. She had an acutely Victorian contempt for a man who left his wife, merely because he happened to have fallen in love with another woman. Since she had never loved anyone or been loved by anyone herself, she did not believe in the power of erotic attraction. She took it for weakness, and how was she going to take a man seriously who was prey to such a weakness. She saw Bertrand Russell's divorce through her friend's eyes, and it would never for a moment have occurred to her that the man had felt the lack of anything in this marriage. This left him as a sinner in her view, and since—unlike her—he was on the short side, a small sinner at that. Bernard Shaw was a different proposition entirely, someone, like herself, uninterested in sex, who thought there were more important things to talk about, and talked about them accordingly. But she was very alert, and noticed right away how, on this very first visit of mine, Aymer and I pricked up our ears each time the name Bertie passed her lips. Aymer, who needed certainty, had to make sure that the man in question was actually Bertrand Russell. "He wouldn't come to you in the Ritz, he's got other fish to fry." "He'll come at the drop of a hat, if *I* ask him," she replied. "He still feels guilty on Alice's account. I treat him like a bootblack in the hotel. Would you like to witness it for yourselves?" she asked, almost innocently. I was duly shocked, at first pro forma, but then quite genuinely, I couldn't believe it, it seemed awful to ask a man of his stamp expressly to humiliate him in front of other guests. I put this to her very briefly, politely, without censure, since it was my first time. Aymer backed me up, not that he necessarily agreed with me, and added: "Perhaps it would be better if there were no other guests present, especially no-one older, so that he would not have to feel quite so humiliated." "Very well," said Mrs Phillimore. "We'll have an evening for the four of us, the two of you, Bertie and me. When are you free?" Aymer, who was never doing anything, liked to play hard to get, and suggested an evening in a fortnight's time. "Donc," said Mrs Phillimore, and when we both pointed out that surely we would have to wait and see whether and when *he* could make it, she laughed sardonically and said: "If *I* ask him, he'll come *tomorrow*." "Shouldn't you ask his wife as well?" "No, he knows that. I've refused to acknowledge any of his wives since Alice. Anyway, he happens not to have one at the moment. He's just left the third, and there's no fourth as yet."

She knew what she was talking about. Except for her ghost stories, I never caught her telling any untruths. On the evening she (or rather Aymer) had selected, he was there, we found him already ensconced when we arrived, a very short man, who, in spite of his age, held himself terribly erect, with a thoroughly intellectual face, his conversational English like that of an educated gentleman of the eighteenth century. He spoke in roughly the style in which Horace Walpole wrote his letters. Mrs Phillimore, whose customary tone was gently teasing, didn't depart from it all evening. She wanted him and us to notice how utterly she despised him for his "immoral" life. Aymer, who was enchanted by his highly intelligent, animated conversation (it was what he most aspired to for himself, and he was capable of it too, aside from the stammering that sometimes came over him at critical points), did not set aside his own social prejudice for a moment. Russell came from the English aristocracy, he was the grandson of a famous prime minister, and had declined to wear his ducal title. Aymer was a mere baronet, though of a very old family while his mother was the daughter of a duke, one of the Northumberland Percys, and, while he was open-minded and objective about many things, he esteemed hierarchy, for all his mockery of his neighbours, whose estates he sometimes visited, it mattered to him that everyone took their own status seriously, and did not seek to deny it in front of others. Aymer's mother had early imbued him with a dislike of this recusant duke. Instead of allowing himself to become, as he ought to have done, the Duke of Bedford, he merely wanted to be the philosopher Bertrand Russell, and he had even gone so far as having himself put in prison for six months for being a pacifist during the First World War.

That evening the talk was not of his beliefs and principles. He had set them out in many well-written and highly readable books. There would have been no point in expressing his convictions about free love at Mrs Phillimore's dinner table. In that respect, she had all the Victorian prejudices, and she was determined not to countenance any of his "amoral" views. He was cheerful, and spoke of literary subjects. Every word came out of his mouth sonorous and well formed, it was clearly articulated, there was none of the lazy mumbling that is so prevalent among educated Englishmen. People said he had taken classes in rhetoric; well, if he had, they were worth it. He was presently working on a collection of stories that later came out under the ironic, provocative title, *Satan in the Suburbs*. Since there was a writer in attendance, he tried it out on the company that evening. In his mouth, English sounded as serene and immaculate as one might expect it from the great writers of the eighteenth century. But he ended his speech with a goat-like laugh that was so wild and dangerous as to be shocking. He refused to end it, drew it out, one could sense how hard it was for him to part with this laughter. Even Mrs Phillimore, who must have known him well, was shocked by it. All the animalism in his nature was expressed in this laugh, a very small, but energetic and indefatigable satyr. This laugh made a curious trinity with the piercing malice of Mrs Phillimore's eyes and the helpless stammer of Aymer. Confronted with so much animalism, I felt a little lame and excluded. There was nothing left for me but to tell a few stories, and one, about the Spanish Duke Dantin and the stolen locomotive, enchanted him to such a degree that he several times said: "You delight me!" with full emphasis. That too, so directly, was something I had never yet heard from any Englishman.

I had run into Duke Dantin when he was a refugee in Paris, during the Spanish Civil War, he had fled from the Republicans, bringing nothing with him except a locomotive, and asked me—we had just been introduced by a mutual friend in a café—whether I knew anyone who might be interested in a locomotive, "*una locomotora*". He had the face of a tiger, in a scaled-down version, and, having made the offer of the locomotive, added in the same breath, that he was going to shoot his brother in Madrid, a traitor. This brother, a famous geographer, had set aside his title of nobility, called himself Dantin Sereseda, and was a Professor at the University of Madrid. He was on the Republican side, and had stayed in Madrid. My new acquaintance regretted his flight on just one ground, namely that he had not got around to shooting his brother first. It had been the last wish of his dying mother that he shoot his brother, that miserable Republican son of hers. He was penniless, but with the help of the locomotive he would get by. As soon as he had sold it, he wanted to get over to Venezuela. He had a friend in the government there, and he would take a ministerial position from him, and as soon as he had embezzled enough money, he would head back to Spain, liberated Spain. Perhaps he would be able to shoot his brother then.

I did not know anything of his subsequent history. As suddenly as he had appeared to my friend, armed with a personal letter of recommendation, as suddenly he disappeared again. With her help, he had been able to sell the locomotive. It was standing in a siding, not far from Versailles, where it could be inspected.

Perhaps it was not just the locomotive as fugitive encumbrance, but the quarrel between the two aristocratic brothers that so enchanted Bertrand Russell about the story. He relaxed a little now, he felt that there was at least *one* member of the little company who was not his enemy, and even though the precision of his eloquence was unchanged, he contrived to suggest that there were many extraordinary tales he might have told. It was clear that he wanted to accredit himself to the one author present on the basis of his forthcoming collection, *Satan in the Suburbs*. A man who had distinguished himself with so many lucid books on the most various subjects—quite apart from his logical-mathematical *chef d'oeuvre*—who had, for instance, following a trip to China, written the best book about it at the time, a man so well informed, and yet so eminently capable of metamorphosis, took this latest one of his into a belletristic writer so seriously that he wanted to impress someone of that ilk, who had no other claim to fame.

We stayed a long time, and all left the hotel together. Aymer allowed himself one last token of disapproval, by not asking Bertrand Russell whether he might run him home—but the old man was not in the least put out, and before our eyes skipped down the steps to Green Park underground station.

Aymer became exaggeratedly polite, insisted that I sit in his Bentley, which he loved more than anything, and, while he drove me up to Hampstead, was told a few home truths about himself.

I met Bertrand Russell once more, but this time in a large group, among many people. The magazine *Nineteenth Century*, which was trying to re-launch itself by the simple expedient of calling itself *Twentieth Century*, was throwing a large party in a house in Mayfair, that had been hired for the occasion. People were invited to meet Mr Pannikar, the Indian Ambassador to China, who had enjoyed a ringside view of events during the years following the revolution, and was now retiring from his post. A trained historian, Mr Pannikar was in the process of writing a book about his experiences. There was an opportunity to meet him, and ask questions. He was a civil and polite gentleman, prepared to speak on anything we had to put to him.

Bertrand Russell, who had published his own book on China a quarter of a century before, was there, and I stood near him as he spoke to Pannikar. It was the most exhaustive interrogation I have ever witnessed. The dialogue came thick and fast, Pannikar was no less quick on his feet than his interlocutor. In the space of twenty minutes, provided you paid attention, and did not allow yourself to be distracted, you learned more than you could have done from reading a thick tome. The questions overlapped and, in the most extraordinary way, light was shed on matters that were not explicitly talked about. These things were so illuminated by what was said before and afterwards, that you could swear you had heard them talked about. There was something about the flighty spirit of Bertrand Russell that allowed the Indian to appear distinguished. He was certainly no-one to be despised, I read his book later, but this questioning was really something else. It turned a clever, methodical and experienced man into a profound thinker. It lifted him, so to speak, from the obligations of ordinary logical connections. What was lost in terms of order was gained in spontaneity. One had the impression that Pannikar was driven to think for the first time about the things he was talking about. That could not in fact have been the case. But thanks to Russell's zigzag leaps and bounds, it had to appear that way. Trivial and everyday things, things that a newspaper reader might have known, didn't even crop up. An "innocent" listener, who merely read a decent newspaper—and there were always such in England—would have had no idea what was going on. Some others had noticed what was going on, and clustered round the two men, listening intently. The cream of the intellectual and political society of London was there. I think all those listening held their breath, they were as rapt as I was. My own response was only more apparent than theirs, because—not being English—I made no effort to dissemble it.

But I had not immediately plunged into the heart of this evening. Before that, I had wandered round various rooms, perhaps to scout out who was there. But possibly I was a little on the lookout for Bertrand Russell, because I had read *his* book about China, which had taught me much, many years before. Suddenly I heard the cackle of the goat, so loud that I took fright, it could only be him. I went in the direction of the cackle, and found him just as he was beginning his dialogue with Pannikar. I did not know what had caused him to whinny so loud and long, because now he got his teeth into the conversation, which took his full concentration for certainly twenty minutes. As it came to an end, it unbent a little, I could tell from the way that only now did I begin to scrutinise the people who had formed a tight ring around the two talkers. I didn't get very far with my research, because quite close to Bertrand Russell, diagonally behind him, stood a strikingly beautiful young woman, whom I had noticed on my first wandering round the rooms, a while before the familiar cackling made itself audible. There were quite a few beautiful women at this gathering. (The beauty of upper class Englishwomen is something that had already struck Dostoevsky, more than a century ago, when he paid a short visit to Alexander Herzen in London.) Every generation was represented, they belonged to powerful or famous men, who had every reason to show themselves with these women on their arms, but this one, who was standing so close to Bertrand Russell that she almost touched him, a little over twenty, was by far the most beautiful. It would be tempting to describe her, but she vanished too quickly. No sooner had Russell put his last question than he sensed her behind him, and quickly turned around. One could tell from his expression that he had never seen her before, he immediately burst out into the goatish laughter, so loud that Pannikar's answer was quite engulfed by it, and no-one heard what it was. Then, as if they had had an assignation, they promptly left together, the eighty-year-old and the twenty-year-old. As he left, he continued to laugh, while she became more beautiful with every stride.

ARTHUR WALEY

He was a connoisseur of Chinese and Japanese and several other Oriental languages, how many exactly, no-one knew. He must have translated two dozen volumes from these languages, mainly from the Chinese. He was a poet himself, and translated in quite a different manner to the way it was done before. The book of songs ... the Chinese *Shih-ching*, a collection of folk songs that Confucius had edited, read in his translation like an authentic collection of folk songs. As they were written in the earliest Chinese period, one may say that they are among the oldest folk songs that are still read and sung today. In no Asian language that I know of is there a translation that can be compared with Waley's. In terms of their poetic substance, one might think of the German collection, *Des Knaben Wunderhorn*. In the equivalence of each one of the 305 poems it contains, in the unity of tone, in the pregnancy of expression and the tempering of still very palpable feeling, I do not know what to set beside it. Waley has also translated poets from the Classical era in China, one of his books deals with one of the great poets of the Tang Dynasty, Po-Chu I. It includes hundreds of his poems, and offers a biography of the poet, as gripping as if it had been of some contemporary of ours. That accounts for two of his twenty-five books. I'll add a third, because it treats of Chinese philosophers, and their anticipation at many points of our "modern" thought. *Three Ways of Thought in Ancient China* contains a first section on Chuang-Tsu, the Taoist, for me the most wonderful thing Chinese civilisation has produced; a second section on Meng-Tsu, whom the Jesuits called Mencius, the most appealing and influential of Confucius' students. The third part hit me like a club, I had never known about the Chinese school of Realist philosophers, as Waley calls them, a precise school of *power*, which had some influence on the creation of the first centralised Chinese empire. It's hard to have any idea of the wonderful readability of these books in good modern prose. This last book appeared in 1939, half a year before the War began. I had reached England a few months before. It was one of the first books I read there. From my very first day in England, it had been my intention to devote myself exclusively to the work on *Crowds and Power*. Nothing else counted, no "literature" was allowed. I was set on denying myself everything that might possibly distract me. And so, as if to reward me, I ran into this book almost right away. I would include it among the ten books that had the greatest significance for me in my life.

By chance, Arthur Waley was the only Englishman who had read anything of mine. Among the "common or garden" languages he had mastered, in addition to his Oriental tongues, was German. He was—such already existed—a passionate skier, and went to Kitzbühl every year at the end of winter. In 1936, he stayed there past Easter. In the Easter issue of the *Frankfurter Zeitung* appeared the first serious article about my novel *Die Blendung* (*Auto da Fé*), which had appeared in autumn 1935. He could not help being struck right away, from reading the review, that the hero of the book was a sinologist. He ordered a copy of the book, and learned that this sinologist had views on women which rather closely matched his own.

He, who rejected most European literature, liked this book, because of the ". . ." of its prose, which reminded him of Chinese. That's what he told me about it, later on.

Perhaps the reader can try to imagine what it meant to me, to be in a great country that to me was the land of Shakespeare and Dickens, and to have *one single* reader. That this reader was a man of the stamp of an Arthur Waley, a man of the most universal culture I had thus far encountered anywhere, didn't make the matter any easier to grasp. It would be to distort our relationship, if I didn't mention this context for it.

We met while the War was still going on, I visited him sometimes in Gordon Square, Bloomsbury, where his library was at the top of the house. In the middle of the room was the long, loaded, but clearly well-organised table, and that was where he did his work.

It began a little one-sidedly, because I was the one who asked questions. I gobbled up his books, of which, thank God, there were many. Each of them was written in finely honed language, as fascinating for poets as scholars, he never repeated anything he had said elsewhere, one learned more and more, and it was this culture that drew me to him most. So it seemed a great stroke of luck that this variously interested man happened to know a book of mine, and to take it seriously. He had a very fine head, not quite a raptor's, but masterful at distance. Nothing said in his presence escaped him, and yet you might suppose he was listening to some faraway sound. The contradiction noted here expresses exactly what one felt in his presence. For the head always seemed half averted, as though attuned to distant movements, which he must remain aware of, and that were within range of him, but only of him. But the notion that he was bored, and wasn't listening, was completely misplaced. Suddenly, and with cutting edge, his answer came to a question, came so quickly that he couldn't have had any time to consider it, and sometimes it even seemed as though he answered before you had asked. More than once I caught myself thinking he could read my mind, and could formulate his answer before I my question. But at the same time the mighty head was listening— I liked to think—to the sounds of Chinese words that didn't have anything to do with the subject of our conversation.

I had never before encountered this sort of double-presence. It surprised me without confusing me, maybe I exaggerated the friendliness of his attitude to begin with, maybe he just enjoyed giving explanations when he was so tirelessly questioned. Since I myself only rarely made any assertions . . . I didn't want to hear anything I knew already when I was in his presence, that would have struck me as a foolish waste of time and a visit. Because, for all interest in oriental matters, everything passed off with English punctuality. The time was portioned out, one mustn't misuse anyone's time, least of all one's own. At first, we would meet for an hour at a time, it was almost as if I'd been taking tuition. Then it grew to an hour and a half, if we were on our own and dining together, never longer. So—quite against my own nature, which in this is oriental—I called time: I looked at my watch—it seems ridiculous to say so, but I did— even when the conversation was most fascinating to me, I got up, he let me go—in England, no-one will ever detain someone making to leave, it would be to meddle in his personal freedom—and felt like an idiot as I walked downstairs, because I was complicit in this awful English habit of husbanding little bits of time.

So I knew him for quite a long time already, without

remarking the contempt he had for many things, just because they meant something to others.

Arthur Waley's arrogance was an arrogance of judgement. He rejected pretty well everything. Anyone unprepared for him could get an awful shock when they encountered his arrogance. Veza met him just once, at a party of Engel Lund's. She had heard a lot about him, in particular, of course, from me, and was looking forward to talking to him about English and German writers. Waley never changed, his expression was always the same, like a Japanese actor's mask, his judgements always came with the same sharpness. They were never adjusted to the capacity of his interlocutor. It was a matter of indifference to him if his death sentence on a cherished author—someone who provided perhaps much-needed solace or support—plunged the reader into incomprehension and dejection. Veza had many such authors, each of them was equally dear to her, and her enthusiasm for them seemed to grow from year to year, perhaps because not enough that was new and sustaining came along to replace it. Whenever she spoke about novels, she always meant characters. She was animated by them, as by close friends, who grew more important with the years. Waley's judgement was levelled at the craft or the mechanics. He never allowed himself to be completely overpowered by characters. He took himself too seriously for that to happen.

The chain of misunderstandings began with *Vanity Fair*. Waley ended any conversation about Thackeray as soon as it began. There was a name that wasn't even unspeakable, it was unmentionable. A blow to Veza, who loved her Becky Sharp. She was immediately thrown, while he behaved as though he hadn't noticed anything, but that was precisely what he was about; the establishment of a sort of rule of terror on the part of judgement. Veza tried this and that, but before long had turned to her *summum bonum*: *Faust*. But there too she was unlucky. "Very bad writing," said Waley. Veza thought she hadn't heard him aright. "Do you mean the students' bouts-rimés?" she asked. "They're masterly." "I mean the lot," came Waley's sharp and swift retort, "no good, no good at all!" I knew Veza would be reeling now. I stood next to her, and felt sorry for her, as indeed I might, she didn't often accompany me to parties. This time, she had allowed herself to be talked into it, because the English translation of *Die Blendung* (*Auto da Fé*) was being celebrated. Waley was the only man in England who had read *Die Blendung* before the War: he had read the original. He had been very impressed, which rarely happened with contemporary writing, and when he met any émigrés, he asked them about the author. He told them in his trenchant fashion that, apart from Kafka and *Die Blendung*, he disdained all German writing. With that judgement, he had swiftly won Veza's heart, even though she thought quite differently of modern German literature. In point of fact, she didn't like Kafka, and enjoyed Thomas Mann. *Die Blendung* was certainly not her favourite book, but it was by me, someone whose fortunes as a writer she pursued with a tenacity bordering on obsession. But she had never been able to lose the suspicion that Kien's hatred for women, had some deep, indirect connection with herself. Therefore, she allowed herself to be persuaded to come to Engel's party, and hoped for a nice conversation with Waley, in which she could show that not only was she well read, but that she understood quite a bit about literature.

She had never dreamed that every name she came up with would be contemptuously tossed back at her, and that, almost rigid with shock, she would so soon be reaching for *Faust*, her trump. She tried Heine, who was graciously conceded to her, not wholeheartedly, but even so, some of his things were just about readable. Dickens was "no good at all". When she crazily mentioned *Les Misérables*, he didn't even bother to reply. She felt herself disintegrate in his eyes, and swiftly moved on to the Russians. That had always seemed to be the safest ground. Tempestuously, she named her favourite novel, *Anna Karenina*. He gestured dismissively, and condescended to utter two words: "Pretty boring." She did not know what to do. I knew Veza would never be able to forgive him. She did not forget it with me either: when she was in a temper, I always got to hear that I too had found *Anna Karenina* pretty boring. She was unshakeably convinced of herself there. It was about the fate of *woman*, and she was certain she was right, in the teeth of Waley's arrogance, or mine.

Perhaps it would have been enough just to quote the conversation between her and Waley, especially all the many names, and a commentary would have been superfluous. But I have only retained some of the names, and I don't want to give any that I'm unsure of. Therefore, I have supplied a few comments on Veza, and on Walcy as well, and resolve to try and be more disciplined in what follows.

Anna Mahler had also turned up at this party, wearing an enormous hat. She only stayed a short while. Once everyone had seen the hat, and touched what was underneath it, she spun round one last time on her own axis, and vanished. She didn't so much as look at Waley, whose coming had been awaited with curiosity and respect, and who was watched in the same manner. It was enough for her to know that, thanks to the hat, she had been noticed by him. But there, she was mistaken, he had no use for women, and had only spoken to Veza because she was standing next to me, and I forced her upon him as my wife.

DIANA SPEARMAN

When I remember England, I always think of the people with whom I had detailedly insipid conversations. There are a good number of them, my life there at that time was largely made up of such conversations. For a lot of people, I became a sort of addiction they weren't able to resist. But I was just as addicted myself, because I was always ready to plunge into hour after hour of these conversations. I listened closely for a long time, I was very scrupulous about that always, but it wasn't just manners, it was my passion to hear whatever people wanted to tell me. In so doing, I behaved just like that class of person I most deeply despise: I was like an analyst, because, while analysts manage to *appear* full of curiosity, they don't really manage much more than patience. They give the appearance of listening. They're good at it, because if you think what they usually have to say for themselves in response, it seems mechanical and predetermined. In reality, their patience consists of the ability to hear the words they have to hear, and swallow them without chewing. They are surely capable of digesting anything, but seriously to contemplate doing so would take up too much of their time. And their time is precious, and they sell it dearly.

I, then, was more a listener than an analyst, and I was given so much to listen to, that I could fill hundreds of volumes with it, if I could remember it. Even the portion that I did remember was sufficient for several books. But I wouldn't even think of going to such a source. All I am interested in is having a few people come to life that at that time became characters to me, and have remained so, even though I haven't thought about them for decades. I want to free myself of this excess of English personalities. But I will only choose those that seem to me typical. I would like them, put together, to make up a portrait of England as it was in the middle of the century.

I'll begin pretty near the top, with Diana Spearman, the ex-wife of a Conservative Member of Parliament, who took a lively interest in her husband's political career. I know nothing about *his* family, he left her, and I never did meet him. Diana's mother was a Howard. She looked like a woman in an Elizabethan miniature—a restrained and concentrated face, not so much intellectual as marked by power, either because one had it, like the originals of many of these miniatures, or else one craved it, as was the case with Diana. She lived in Lord North Street, a short street very close to the Houses of Parliament, where mainly politicians lived. There, she would give intimate dinner parties for six or eight people, so that proper conversation was possible, and you actually got to know most of the people. They were people of name and substance, mostly Conservative politicians, who were glad of her hospitality when they were in opposition, and later on, when their names meant more to the general public, kept their faith with her. In amongst them was the odd writer or scientist. She herself wrote books on literary or political subjects, though she had no interest in modern literature per se. What she did know a lot about was English literature of the eighteenth and nineteenth centuries, which is such a rich field, that merely by reading that and nothing else, one can become a fairly complete human being.

Her dinners were conducted in some style. People only spoke about things and persons that they really knew something about. Even though the majority, perhaps even all, of what was said came out of some prejudice or other, it was brought forth in a form that stimulated discussion and riposte. The most important thing was not to show off. Any element of show or claim to preeminence was avoided. Even the most distinguished guest replied kindly and thoughtfully to every question from some possibly wholly unknown guest. Foreigners were invited too, up to a point. Celebrated foreigners, or such of whom one might assume they would one day become celebrated. The other guests treated them with particular attentiveness. No-one who came and dined here would ever have thought that of all nationalities, the English are the one that most deeply rejects foreigners.

Many of the guests, who were in the hurly-burly of public life, were well informed about the political scene. But they appeared relaxed, and the prevailing tone was open. Maybe someone could have come away with all sorts of secret or privileged information, but of all the many times I was a guest at Diana's table, there was only one occasion when I sensed suspicion, from one of her oldest friends, Richard Law, universally known as Dick Law, one of Churchill's "young men", who, at the time I met him, was Lord Coleraine. It was a time of political tension, a lot of confidential matters were discussed, and I could tell my presence troubled Richard Law, he stopped once in mid-sentence, looked at me sceptically, he was almost at the point of asking Diana who I was and what I was doing there. Of course, he didn't do that, but he let me know that he was unwilling to be open in the presence of someone of whom he knew nothing, and especially someone who was listening so attentively. He must have felt my intensity, he had it himself, he was certainly a man of passionate convictions, not your common-or-garden politician, and certainly not as smooth and glib as many others. I made no attempt to dissemble how keenly I was listening, and even though I had different views to him on practically every subject, I liked him, and he spoke as though he meant what he said (something one isn't often moved to say of such gatherings). If it didn't sound quite so ridiculous, I should have to say that I was always a spy, a spy who followed all the various types of humanity, and wherever I saw a particular type, then I listened with even greater attention than usual. He, though, who lived and breathed politics, could only conceive of such intensity as that of a spy. At Diana's I met many people from public life, and spent many evenings at dinner-table conversations, quite often the same ones. But that was the only occasion on which I encountered suspicion, something for which I, a suspicious nature myself, have a particularly keen sense. Law wasn't the least bit interested in my opinions, no wonder really, as he must have thought they were window-dressing anyway.

I should mention them all by name, all those Conservative politicians I ran into there, there were many interesting characters among them, but the most interesting among them— certainly, the most striking—was Enoch Powell.

ENOCH POWELL

Diana had told me about him. He was an MP. She talked about him with particular pride, because he was one of only two Tory MPs from humble backgrounds. That was an important matter for the Conservatives, at a time when the Labour party was in government. Naive and inexperienced as I was in English matters, I imagined a couple of men from working-class families, and was very much surprised when I met Enoch Powell at her house. He wasn't at all the son of a labourer, maybe a teacher, but what immediately struck me about him was the Continental, one might almost say Central European way he presented himself. He straightaway broached Nietzsche and Dante with me. Dante he quoted in Italian, and at considerable length. The thing that attracted him about Dante was the explicitly partisan nature of it, the civil war in the population still meant something, it hadn't degenerated to civilities. The civilised tone that prevailed in the House of Commons he disliked. In Dante's day, people were burned at the stake. When the other side came to power, you had to leave the city, and not come back as long as you lived. Hatred of the enemy *burned*. Dante's *Commedia* was full of this, he was a man who neither forgot nor forgave. The great thing about his poetry in particular was that he forgot nothing.

I listened to him with fascination. This wasn't a tone I had ever heard in that house before. Enoch Powell had a reputation for being an impassioned speaker in the Commons, and he was no less impassioned in this house. He was, moreover, able to show what he knew, without any false modesty, which he would have been unable to do in Parliament, or anywhere else in English public life. From Dante, he got on to Nietzsche, a very evident model for him. He was a Classicist by training, and knew Latin and Greek so well that, at the age of twenty-five, he had been offered a Professorship at Sydney in Australia. Perhaps that was when his interest in Nietzsche dated from, who was called away to Basle at a similarly young age. I couldn't ask him when and why he had become interested in Nietzsche, but it was clearly important to him, and there was no sign of its having diminished over time. He read him in German, and again quoted great chunks in a somewhat theatrical style for my benefit, since I was able to judge how good his German was, quite as good as his Italian. Because of the presence of other guests, I was too polite to embark on a conversation in German with him. He would certainly have liked to. He gave a meaningful look around, and sighed audibly. None of the guests who were present that evening could speak German. But of course it was more than the language that drew him to Nietzsche, it was the will to power: I don't know that I have ever encountered anyone quite so antithetical to everything I stand for. I didn't express my own opinions. I went to this house to learn about traditional old England, and not to give myself airs, and in this house I learned what people are like when they have exercised power, including world power, for a long time, up to a couple of centuries. Enoch Powell was not thought of as typical. He was as hard-working as a German, and didn't mind being given the most onerous tasks. He spoke several languages without an accent, which is a rare accomplishment indeed in

Britain, and for all his love of the Empire, he did not despise other *white* cultures, and where most educated people here turn to the Romans, he based his own outlook on Dante and Nietzsche.

It was the time just after Churchill had given up India, and Diana told me that Enoch, as she referred to him, had been one of very few MPs who had voted against Churchill. I learned that he had lived in India for many years, and knew it well. The second or third time I met him at Diana's, we left together. Out on the street, our conversation turned to India. The word as he said it sounded plangent, like a lament for someone recently dead. Perhaps more from curiosity than empathy, I asked him: "Are you very upset over the loss of India?" He stopped in the middle of the street, and beat his breast several times: "It hurts, in here!" Now I was the one to feel stricken. His outburst, theatrical by English standards, was nonetheless genuine. He hesitated before we went on, he would have liked to say more, but he must have considered that he didn't know me at all well, and that I wasn't perhaps the right person with whom to share his deepest feelings. Because that was certainly what they were. These feelings ultimately joined forces with his ambition, and, in the course of the next few years, were to make him a leading proponent of racialist politics.

In the War, he had been a brigadier in Montgomery's desert army, and had distinguished himself by his bravery. He had also acquired various knowledge that belongs to the upper-caste Englishman, but which he couldn't have had before on account of his humble background. He once spoke to me about one of those important matters: it was fox-hunting. In the English translation of *Crowds and Power*, which he read with the professional interest of a man ambitious for power, he had encountered the category of packs. Among these, he had been especially impressed by the hunting packs, and he told me how much he had learned in this practice during the War, of value for his subsequent life in England. I think he was familiar with funeral crowds from his time in India, but we didn't talk further about that. What was important to him, because it was one of the tools of the trade of the Conservative politician, so to speak, was the fox hunt.

Not long after, there came a time when his speech against coloured immigrants caused a stir, and made him one of the most popular politicians of the day. He predicted fearful consequences if immigration policy was not forcibly halted. Rivers of blood would flow—and with that hearts flew to him, those of workers and the salt of the earth, natural Labour supporters, dockworkers and butchers in their thousands flocked to Parliament, and demonstrated for Enoch Powell. Thousands and thousands of approbatory letters were delivered to him, it was all anyone could do just to count the sacks of them. When I went to get my hair cut in Baker Street, the hairdresser, whom I had known for years, would greet me—and this was most unlike him—with the loud cry: Enoch Powell, that was the only politician he could trust to speak for him. I was beside myself at this turn of events in England. In this instance, I happened to know the genesis of a demagogue, it was a man who had grown up quoting from Dante and Nietzsche.

VERONICA WEDGWOOD

I met Veronica during the War, through Friedl. As an editor at Jonathan Cape, Veronica had taken up the cause of Friedl's novel, *Let Thy Moon Arise*, and gone to visit her in Downshire Hill. Friedl told her about her "teacher", and the way she talked about it, her absolute devotion to this teacher made a great impression on Veronica. Perhaps she also wanted to get to know the model of Friedl's novel, which had struck her as being very original. She borrowed a copy of *Die Blendung* from the British Museum, and, as her German was very good, set about reading it. Ever since then, she was obsessed with Kien and his fate, perhaps Friedl's obsession had transferred itself to her. At any rate, she decided that *Die Blendung* would have to come out in English, and she began to badger Jonathan Cape, her boss. The moment she had succeeded in convincing him and his publishing colleagues, she wrote me a fine and dignified letter, in which she communicated to me the firm's offer for the book. We met in the garden at 35 Downshire Hill, in Friedl's presence.

Friedl was a bright and cheerful creature, with a very pronounced sense of humour. There was always something to laugh about when we were together, but on this occasion, when she was introducing Veronica to her teacher, of whom she had always spoken in the loftiest and most exalted terms, there was an almost ceremonial atmosphere. Veronica was short and dark and a little on the heavy side, not at all your usual Englishwoman. She explained her appearance by her Celtic forebears. She was very quick on the uptake, remembered everything, reacted sharply; in England, where there are so many stodgy people, she was certainly the very opposite, someone with whom you could never be bored. But she was never confident of her effect on others, and always had the feeling of not being taken seriously. Emotional serenity fascinated her and, like Friedl, she would gladly have submitted to a man she idolised, but she wasn't physically attractive, her face was too broad and flat, her expression piteous, her movements rather graceless, but her voice was warm and rich and sonorous. If one had heard her only, perhaps then one might have fallen in love with her, and, as I gradually learned, there was in fact more than one man who had fallen for the charms of her voice and her background. But they weren't men of the kind she was looking for, she admired great historical figures: William the Silent, Strafford, Monmouth, she followed them out to their battlefields, which she explored, she read their letters and memoirs, she lived, much more than is usual for historians, *their lives*, vicariously. She had an instinct for passion and certainty, and I think it was that that most impressed her when she saw Friedl and me together that first time.

I had become used to adopting a harsh tone with Friedl. I wanted her to work, I thought she was very gifted. But she was also incredibly lazy, and it was a real effort to get her to work. I rarely praised her, only when she managed to accomplish something that genuinely impressed me. Then she would feel my withdrawing from her—only her, of all people—and today I am sure that she was deeply grateful for the stinginess of my praise, my continual dissatisfaction with her, my rebukes, yes, that was exactly what she needed.

MISERY AT PARTIES

Nowhere did I feel more miserable and solitary than at parties. Veronica Wedgwood's were the worst. There, you would feel there was absolutely nothing right with the world. It wasn't that you were treated sceptically, it was worse than that. You quite simply didn't exist. Before and after a conversation, it was exactly the same. Self-assertion was futile, no-one expected there to be any self to assert. Whoever wasn't already known would certainly not become so. Talking did nothing to change that. It would be an exaggeration to describe the exchange of a few sentences as a conversation and, in any case, the content of a conversation wasn't what mattered, so much as the confirmation of what remained unsaid. What was at issue was observing the proprieties. One mustn't on any account get too near. Edges and boundaries were the important things, and they existed so as not to be infringed. I am unable to give an account of a party at Veronica's. Her own insecurity exacerbated the insecurity of her guests. You were surrounded by an appearance of benevolence, a guarantee perhaps that no-one would tear off a piece of flesh from your body. Generally, you didn't know who you were talking to. A question would have been accounted impolite. Others, whom you might already see as friends, you could ask. There was a great difference between parties at Veronica's, and parties at Kathleen Raine's, say. With the latter, there was still a vestige of studentiness, a hope that you might meet someone who could help you, yes, even a trace of curiosity. The hostess, in either case, was particularly fond of me, so the occasions are strictly comparable. Veronica, from a very good family—the Wedgwoods and Darwins were related—had been born an unwanted child. Her mother had wanted a son, and instead she had had a daughter. She did not really want the child, did not feel any joy when she was born, and she let her know. She was eight, I believe, when she was told. Veronica, who was quick and bright—she had a good brain, and exceptional instincts—therefore never really felt secure. Even after she'd become a famous historian, there was always something imploring, almost wheedling in her voice. Once, at one of her parties, she had just greeted me, she fell down in front of me on the floor. It looked so theatrical that it seemed almost deliberate, which it surely couldn't have been. She was very ambitious, but whether she believed in her ambition, deep down, I still don't know to this day.

With Kathleen Raine, the resolve to make her way in society was everything. You might have supposed that that was all there was to her, even though she was forever talking about great poetry, or, failing that, about Jung. The part played by psychoanalysis of both schools in English society at the time would be something that repaid study. It's not sufficient to say that it was embraced with open arms, no, people gobbled it up or prostrated themselves at its feet. This was a subjection so absolute and so servile as you only get in an established master breed. I felt uncouth if I ever said anything against it. People forgave me, because of course they took me for something of the same sort. The only thing they told one another about me was that I was a patient listener, and would listen to anyone moan for hours. Anyone who was so careless of his own time, and even then was always prepared to meet you another time, if there was something you had to complain about, could only be an analyst, particularly if he happened to come from Vienna.

FRANZ STEINER

Eyes that seemed to be moving incessantly, without it meaning anything, in a face that almost lacked a forehead.

A body so small and frail, it barely existed.

Then the gently plaintive voice, never without that undertone, even when, as often between us, the talk was of some other matter, for instance about hard science. It took me a while to get used to the tone, and then I stopped hearing it, and only became aware of it again when I introduced him to someone new.

Because what he said was always clear and concise, he had more to say than most people. He never disregarded what someone else had said, and he always thought about his own reply. Untidy thinking was repugnant to him, there was something forever searching in his mind, you could depend on his judgements, but you had to get used to his rhythm, which was a little slow and perhaps overly considered.

I liked it best when we were both listening to someone else, whom he or I, each in his own way, would encourage to speak. There was a place where this often happened, and, since it was he who first brought me there, I want to say something about it. It was called Student Movement House.

Franz Steiner. There's so much to say about him. Where to begin?

Franz Baermann Steiner

His life was governed by his form, he had none. He was small and so slight, you could easily overlook him. His face was uncommonly ugly: a high, receding brow, helpless eyes in perpetual agitation. Weepy speech, even where there was nothing particular to complain about. A less attractive person one could scarcely imagine.

But then you started talking to him, and in his slow, seemingly passionless way, he always had something to say. It was always clear and concrete and unrhetorical. It contained what it contained, never any means of projection or amplification. If you were used to the slight plangency of the tone, and were able to disregard it (you couldn't fail to hear it), you began to sense that a further constant presence in this speech was a question, so modestly couched that it seemed not even to want an answer. You had to be somewhat familiar with the intellect of the man to know that these answers would be immense. They are so rarely met with that a sensible person would not even be looking for them.

What you can ask about with impunity are laws. They are fixed in their formulation, and finally it is all some people can do to ask after the formulation of these laws. And that was Franz Steiner's style. More and more he decided for the law-abidingness of his belief.

But he never made any attempt to convert me. He never dared interfere with the drive for freedom that governed my nature. He was, rather, grateful that in spite of his growing confinement to a historically defined faith, I took him as seriously as if he'd been free, as free as I must certainly feel myself.

In a way he would certainly never have admitted in the later years of our friendship, he was free. He was free in his myths. He was the only man I knew with whom I could speak about myths. Not only did he know a great number of them, and could as easily surprise me with one as I him; he didn't interfere with them, he didn't interpret them, he made no effort to order them scientifically, he let them be. For him, they never became mere means to an end. They were the highest and most precious thing that humanity has created for itself. We could talk about myths together for days on end, each of us came up with new ones that he offered the other, and always they had been the essential thing for some group of people, always had had validity and currency and force. Neither of us in these conversations would have dared to invent anything.

We talked about myths that had been scrupulously handed down, myths by which people regulated their lives, never some playful invention of his or mine. The trust between us was based on respect for the myths over which each of us separately spent a large portion of his time. It might seem that this isn't all that unusual, but then one would overlook the fact that almost all experts in mythology misuse them for some other ends, to sustain or support certain theories or distinctions.

Innocent respecters and observers of myths are rare. Even among poets, I have only known those who had this innocence on a temporary basis, usually in the making of some work on which they were engaged.

His feeling for what life ought to be. His calm and luminous understanding of it. It was unattainable for him, he *dreamed* of it. He dreamed of having a family, a wife and children. He loved his sister, whom he lost early. The mark of his confidence in me was when he showed me a picture of this sister. All the women he later pursued with such indescribable patience were like his sister. For others, whom he might have won—irrespective of his ugliness— he had only contempt. It made him angry if people took trouble over him, never perhaps realising how much he radiated help-lessness. In his notion of a family, he was the *man*, and he was furious with any woman who tried to baby him. I have to say something about the outer man, to understand why he was never able to achieve something as ordinary as a family.

He died just as a woman became engaged to him. This was the British writer Iris Murdoch, who knew him at Oxford, and had been intellectually vanquished by him. She gave him the manuscript of her first novel. For years, he had been threatened by a serious heart condition, and he was reading it even as a final attack came upon him. The last letter he wrote to me was about this novel: he asked me passionately, which he would never otherwise have done, to read this novel. It was *Under the Net*, and he must be called the true discoverer of Iris Murdoch.

She resembled his sister. On his sickbed, he asked her to be his wife. She accepted, and saw herself as his fiancée. His heart condition was terminal. But it is possible that it was his joy at becoming engaged that led to his death. In this way, he, who was always unhappy, at least died happy.

Steiner had a great love of truth and never flattered. Veza, who was a wild flatterer, must have seemed extraordinary to him. His love of beauty was such that nothing he said to a woman could appear to him as flattery, he always believed it.

His "Prayer in the Garden on my Father's Birthday", which I reread yesterday—after forty years—moved me greatly. It was written under the influence of Jorge Manrique, and never was any influence more legitimate.

Steiner would have loved to visit Spain with me, and as far as I was concerned, he went there for me.

His letters from Spain are among the most beautiful he wrote to me.

In our conversations about peoples—among them many so-called primitive peoples—my emphasis was on the mythology, his on early poetry. In his letters, he would often copy out poems from tribes he was studying, myths, never, so far as I remember, or only rarely. He attributed to me a power of persuasion for which he envied me. Before long, he made bold to use it on his own behalf. Since he only ever wooed seriously—he wanted to marry and start a family, that was what he most, and almost incessantly, thought about—he could see nothing facile about engaging as an advocate someone who admired him, who knew his intellectual worth and his reliability, and was able to talk about these qualities to the parties in question, with the fire he didn't himself have.

He didn't know better than words, and he did not always try to reach behind words. He was free of psychoanalysis. He could receive a suggestion from there, weigh it up coolly and critically, without necessarily succumbing to it. Weighing things up was his thing. Poetry for him was a weighing of words. He never read anything without writing down the words he liked. The fact that he did this in many languages, including those he approached from outside, as an anthropologist, did nothing to rob the German words he wrote in of their validity. It was not possible for him to waste or disfigure something precious like a word. He spoke slowly and haltingly, he had always thought about what he said. You were never close to a source when you listened to him, but you were close to a final result. Work was an almost hallowed word for him. He got ready to work, he could spend many days preparing himself. He dreamed of places and rooms that were good for working in, he felt them as workscapes, so to speak, without congratulating himself for mere industry.

It offended him that I would only answer every third or fourth letter from him. A regular correspondence was hard for me, to me letters were like outbursts that I had to wait for, I didn't like to compel them.

He knew this, as a good observer, it couldn't have escaped him long, but seeing as he didn't merely live in his letters, but also *wanted* things in them, I was wary of answering his every whim. When complaints were unavailing, he threatened to end our friendship, but when he saw that that didn't help either, he contented himself with having made the threat.

When he came down to London from Oxford in the war years we would meet at Student Movement House on Gower Street. That was a place where students met from all over, from India and Africa, but also from the white dominions. Émigrés came here from every European country, but also Arabs, Chinese, Malays. It was a club without prejudices, the only precondition for acceptance was some connection with the university. Most of the people there were young, but there were others too, who had long since finished their studies. You could get into conversation with anyone at all, you said who you were, took a seat, talked, got up again whenever you felt like it, or if you wanted to talk to someone else. It was the most open, unprejudiced atmosphere I have ever encountered. Of course people remained what they were, but for the hours they spent at the club, they set aside their prejudices quite naturally and easily, their ease remains unforgettable.

Steiner, who had come to England a few years ahead of me, had introduced me to this club. For him as an anthropologist, it was a paradise, and it was the best present he could give me to select this place for our conversations. Whenever his commitments would allow, we would spend three or four hours there together, in serious and intense conversation, interspersed with meetings with the most varied people who approached us, or those he wanted me to get to know. You must imagine what it meant, when we were just talking about Ashanti proverbs, and he stopped to introduce me to Kessi, an Ashanti prince. Not that we learned much about Ashanti proverbs from him, but we could at least picture the people who used them, and if it wasn't the somewhat superciliously smiling Kessi, but another student from the Gold Coast, then such proverbs were used to please us. You could really rely on the wonderful collections put together by British explorers and field workers.

Both he and I liked to surprise the other with a book he might have been looking for in vain for a long time. It became a kind of contest that became essential to our lives. The bookshops around the British Museum were inexhaustible, and as much time as we spent talking we also spent hunting old books. Among all those days of looking, there was one on which I showed Steiner a copy of Bleek and Lloyd's *Specimens of Bushman Folklore*, one of the glories of world literature, which I couldn't live without. I had stumbled upon it, just before our meeting in the club, he couldn't believe his eyes, I held it out to him, he turned the pages with trembling hands, and congratulated me—just as one might congratulate someone on some major life event. There were also wonderful moments when one of us had something to give the other, if it was something he already had in his own collection.

Our conversations were a stimulating mixture of books from all over the world, that we brought with us, and of people from all over the world, who sat around us. There were lawyers among them, future politicians, linguists, anthropologists, historians, philosophers, and one or two doctors. No-one compelled anyone else to take an interest in his own field, but they were all the more happy to be asked detailed questions about it. I have never been in any more intellectually tolerant society. Everyone was taken notice of, even the most shy or reclusive person received interest. Anyone who ordinarily would have been too timid, thawed out here under the tactful curiosity. Of course, there were some who felt compelled to put on a show, but where there were so many others doing the same thing, they soon became inconspicuous or gave up.

Of Steiner himself I have to say that he was never ill-humoured in this place. He, who suffered so much from not having a family, and basically was perpetually bemoaning the fact—here, he was braced, alert, attentive, so compelled or interested by others, that he didn't seem any more unhappy than they were, and didn't for once feel sorry for himself.

DOWNSHIRE HILL

A cosy street of . . . houses that led down from Rosslyn Hill to Hampstead Heath, not a long street, but on the odd-numbered side from 1 to 37, in good condition, and with very few buildings that were not original. The houses normally two storeys high, simple, classically proportioned, the absence of superfluous frippery so agreeable that it was always a pleasure to stroll down it, even when I didn't have any particular business there, wasn't visiting anyone who lived on it. There was a subliminal connection between "Down" and "Hill" that lives strongly in the memory, but this was a street that wasn't merely pleasant to look at, it also had interesting residents. There were some who had been living there as long as I was in Hampstead, for decades, others moved on after a few years. The front gardens were almost non-existent, but one knew that there was a long garden behind each of the houses, and that it was carefully and lovingly tended. Near the bottom end of it, a short street branched off it that was famous all over the English-speaking world, because this is Keats Grove, named after the poet Keats, who lived there for a time at Fanny Brawne's house, and wrote one of the most beautiful poems in English in her garden: his "Ode to a Nightingale". The house had been restored to its original condition, and designated as a museum to Keats. Even during the War, visitors came there from all over the world, and they weren't the worst people

Keats' House, Wentworth Place, Hamsptead

either. Keats suffered from tuberculosis, and died very young in
Rome, not many months after leaving this house, at the age of
twenty-five.

It's true that his name wasn't often used on Downshire Hill.
But he was always present, even during the dictatorship of
Eliot, who arrogantly, almost shamelessly, dismissed all
Romantic writing. I hope he will never be forgiven in particular
for the words he applied to Blake. Keats was a sick young god,
who made himself beloved with his few precious years as a
mortal.

By and by, I got to know many of the houses and inhabitants
of Downshire Hill, either because I was visiting some resident
painter, sculptor or writer, or else because I had close friends
who happened to move into one of these houses. During the
War, the most important house for me was 35, the second to
last. Friedl, my young friend and student, lived there, the house
belonged to her cousin Margaret, who was only occasionally
there during the War, but preferred, especially during

dangerous periods, to live in the Chilterns.

No. 35 was a citadel of modernism. Margaret was a collector of abstract art, which was still a new phenomenon at the time, the galleries seemed to be full of nothing but Gabo, Ben Nicholson and Barbara Hepworth. She was a friend and patron of all three, completely certain of herself as she should be, and convinced also that her collection would appreciate in value, if only she lived for long enough, but not collecting for that reason. Margaret was the daughter of a famous father, the most important Egyptologist of the time, a student with Erman in Berlin, and independently wealthy, so that he could give himself to his pursuit, without needing to look for a chair at a university anywhere. A gentleman scholar, of a sort that was still fairly widespread in nineteenth-century England, Darwin being the best known example. While Margaret's father, Alan Gardiner, was never a professor, still his *Egyptian Grammar* was the basis for the teaching of the language. For decades, it had the reputation for being the best grammar in any language, whether it still has that today I am unable to say. The father of the man who was able to pursue such a happy and successful hobby had himself amassed a large fortune from his coffee (or was it tea?) plantations in Africa, and even Margaret's work as a patroness of the arts was founded on the material success of her grandfather. Her mother Heddi was from Vienna, and Friedl was her niece. Already in Vienna, there was some Finnish blood in the family, both Margaret and her mother had Finnish faces. An old relative of theirs, who translated Dante into Finnish, was still living on a Finnish island into a high old age, a kind of avatar of literary studiousness, I was once able to see her in Vienna.

No. 35 was interesting not only on account of its collection of paintings and sculptures. Still more interesting—to me at least—was the array of its temporary residents and visitors. Margaret offered the use of her house to all sorts of people, who stayed there for long or short periods of time. It would be easy to write a book about the people I met there. When she was there, she gave dinners to which four or six people would be invited, usually people who were used to speaking in public, acknowledged experts in their chosen fields, whether it was science, or . . . one of the arts, from whom one could learn a great deal. Very often, they were people of the left in one form or other, talking for their cause, at loggerheads with the government even during the War, and making the most of their right to free expression. That was the thing that most astonished me about England during the War. I could hardly believe my ears when, following a dazzling speech of Churchill's, Aneurin Bevan would step up and deliver a tirade glowing with impish eloquence against the War. In Parliament, you were untouchable. In Parliament, anyone could say anything. A single individual could speak against 600, and say whatever he wanted to, and he was allowed to. My admiration for this parliamentary system in a world where various leaders of various stripe laid down the law, became inexhaustible. Perhaps that was why, even in the year when England stood alone against a Hitler drunk on victory, I retained my unshakeable conviction that the War would end well; while other émigrés, often the cleverest and the most convinced, for good reason, feared for their lives—a successful invasion, and the occupation of the country would have spelled doom for them—I never felt myself under that threat. Under the best spiritual—and the worst material—conditions, I could devote myself to my work, where slowly and thoroughly, but never doubting, I discussed the varieties of crowds and the ruses of power.

J. D. BERNAL

The visitor I most often saw was the physicist, J. D. Bernal, whose scientific gifts, wide knowledge and political convictions were all equally breathtaking. He was accounted one of those scientists, who, by common consent were thought to be worthy of the Nobel Prize, that only blind chance had kept him from winning. He was interested in everything, not just his own specialism and others related to it, he was a Fellow of the Royal Society, the oldest and still the most respected scientific body in the world. Only two members of the Royal Society belonged to the tiny Communist Party in England, and one of them was him. He had thoroughly studied Marx. Unshakeable in his convictions, still he wasn't tied down like most of the Soviet scientists, forced or bent to some official opinion; he retained his openness and curiosity about everything. He was immediately prepared for a discussion; whomever he met in that house, he was ready for any of their questions. Not only would he explain the most difficult things—with that pedagogical clarity characteristic of English scientists—he would reply patiently to *questions*, and refused to be provoked into impatience or irritation even by stupid people. The most surprising thing for me was the lack of arrogance, a thing so rare, even among highly tolerant English intellectuals, that I hardly believed it at first, and kept trying to test it. Once, I talked to him about mass symbols, mass symbols of nationhood in fact. Nothing could be more antithetical to his experimentally or mathematically founded insights. He listened to me quietly, but not bored at all. For him, I wasn't a nobody, I was some émigré from Vienna, from whom one might thereby expect a line in psychological speculations, even if he had nothing in common with Freud, and in fact often talked against him. Freud (whose books and theories Bernal knew well—almost as well as he knew Marx's theories) enjoyed a very high status in England. What did I have to oppose it? Not a single psychological text, just a novel that hadn't been translated (it was wartime, after all, and the English translation of *Auto da Fé* didn't appear till 1946), but he listened to me, asked sensible, not destructive questions, didn't refer me to this or that view of someone else's, the better to understand my opinions, no, he left me my dignity, without accepting one iota of what I said. At the end of our conversation, which went on for an hour and a half, I wasn't left ashamed, but full of questions for myself. Certainly, it was no more than a skirmish because my ideas were at the time still crystallising, but it left everything open, it was stimulating. To others, he said in a tone of respect: "You know, he's even crazier than . . . ," (another psychological "speculator"). A type of thinking that set out from different premises was, in his eyes, perfectly permissible. He was curious about any intellectual move that wasn't vacuous, and, while others polemicised against you pitilessly, he was quite happy to advance abstruse theories from the history of science that are nowadays thought of as idiotic, even though they were once advanced by great figures like Kepler or Newton. With that, he consciously nettled the sterile arrogance of persons who always proceeded in rigid orthodoxy, while not having done the least thing themselves.

This man was, as already said, a respected member of the English Communist Party, an advocate of its politics, and an abider by its determinations, although I have to say that only a part of his character was obedience, and there was a lot left of him.

"Tolerance" was a virtue among English intellectuals, and the word "virtue" itself is apt here, it was something that was consciously cultivated, just like certain qualities in Greek or Roman philosophy. It was connected to a striving for clear and precise formulation. Anything indistinct was anathema to such people, but the paradox, if expressed sharply enough, enjoyed great popularity. I met scientists at the time whose favourite reading matter were Shaw's "Prefaces". But this tolerance also comprised an immovable arrogance, which for me remained the leading characteristic of the English upper classes. Bernal had not a trace of this arrogance—he was also the only one of them I got to know—and he attributed that to his Irish background. His name was Spanish, and he had an explanation for that too. When the Armada was wrecked by winter storms, some Spanish ships had been forced onto the coast of Ireland. Several hundred Spaniards were able to save their lives, their ships were driven onto the rocks, and a few were able to swim ashore; they stayed in Ireland, while keeping their Spanish names. It was from one of these families—I think it was in County Cork—that Desmond Bernal came.

GEOFFREY PYKE

A man whom Bernal took to be the greatest inventive genius of his time came, through his good offices, to live in the house on Downshire Hill, No. 35. His name was Geoffrey Pyke, and he lived without the least academic duties. He came from a wealthy background, lost his fortune, got himself another by speculating (and calculating the mathematical odds), founded and subsidised a school at which children were educated according to psychoanalytical principles; lost his money all over again over this; got it back through further ingenious speculation; lost it, and this time never got it back. He had a head full of a hundred ideas for new inventions, he and Bernal were friends, and whenever he saw him, he put forward suggestions for fresh inventions. It was the time that Lord Mountbatten had been put in charge of the preparations for the Normandy landings.

Bernal gave Geoffrey Pyke his highest recommendation. Among the stream of his ideas—he came up with new inventions every day—there would certainly be something that might come in handy for the planned landing. Mountbatten gave Pyke a place on his staff of advisers. It was an extraordinary, wholly unbureaucratic arrangement, unthinkable in any other country at war. Geoffrey Pyke lived in a room in 35 Downshire Hill. The décor was Spartan: a bed, a table, a very few chairs, scientific journals in piles all round the room. There he would sit, read, think, invent, he was an invalid and often had to lie down, in pain or not, I don't know. His face was usually clouded. He was tall and dark, a short beard did nothing to detract from his beauty and dignity, he looked like a figure on a Byzantine icon. But no religious thoughts were entertained in that head, it was always full of mathematical and scientific problems, it was as though it never had a moment's rest from such thoughts. Illness didn't make any difference either, if he couldn't make it into the office and stayed at home, then he would be visited by Mountbatten, who, it was said, was unhappy if he didn't have the daily stimulus of a conversation with him. At any rate, he often came by the house, in a dull mood, without any escort. One assumed that very extraordinary or crucial things were then discussed, of which we of course never got to hear anything.

It was only after the War that we learned of the wealth of ideas, some of them seriously considered, others rejected, but there were certainly some that were approved and put into effect. One of Pyke's ideas, which is said to have impressed Churchill, was the use of artificial icebergs for the landing. In the end, nothing came of it. I haven't investigated these matters historically, I'm merely repeating things that were said at the time.

Whenever I went to the house, I would look in on Geoffrey Pyke, who had been living there for more than a year. He was a clever and articulate speaker, who liked to regale me with literary ideas of a satirical-didactic nature. Shaw's Prefaces were his Bible, and he loved quoting from them. Certainly, he made them seem an inexhaustible font. He had Shaw's works in his room, quite a little library of them, and although he must have known the Prefaces inside out, he liked to take down a volume from time to time, and read out a sentence or two. With his memory, this wasn't strictly necessary, but since he was drawn to the more paradoxical utterances, he may have thought they might have an easier passage if he had the sourcebook to hand. His voice had a mellifluous quality that only became apparent when he was quoting from Shaw. It was as though—in this refined way—he was acting as a sort of agent on Shaw's behalf, which, at this time of his greatest fame, Shaw certainly didn't need. It took me a while to understand that what he was doing was the conversational counterpart of his inventions. Shaw's paradoxes were a defence of the originality of his own scientific or technical ideas.

Nothing that was already familiar or established had any authority for him.

He was a solitary. He never had any personal or familial visitors. He had apparently been unhappily married. He never received a lover. Never having been a professor, he had no students. He had a very few friends like Bernal, who didn't speak about his person, but who were in awe of his intellect. I got the impression that Bernal, the widely acknowledged omniscient, rated him more highly than he did himself. We had heard how he had been plundered at the times of his wealth. He had been so open-handed that he had given everything for any undertaking that pleased or impressed him intellectually.

Friedl, who stayed in the house throughout the War, was an agreeable presence for Geoffrey Pyke. She was bright and cheerful, often exuberant, and, in spite of that, fascinated by people. She liked to get him in conversation, often in the doorway, when she had made something to eat down in the kitchen, and asked him whether he would like some. Usually he would refuse, he had some idea he was working on, and didn't want to be disturbed. But there were other times when he wouldn't want to eat, but was happy to chat. Then there would be a torrent of ideas about Shaw, or some comparable idea of his own. Friedl listened, you couldn't interrupt him. She was mesmerised by his voice, and his paradoxes made her laugh. Without any access to science herself, she could still sense his mind and his inventiveness. Then, after about ten minutes, he would suddenly interrupt himself, and she would step away. He never asked her into his room. When he was lying ill in bed, he would allow food—very little—to be brought to him. But, as she said, he always kept his frontiers. His suspicion of women, following the coming to grief of his marriage, was insuperable. But he loved her laugh, and—a sign of his highest trust—once told her: "You are like a child. It's impossible to be angry with you, even if you bother me."

When his consultative role was over—the War had been won—he went back to being so poor that he couldn't afford to pay any rent. He was so proud that he never asked anyone for anything. When someone, knowing of his importance, offered him the use of a room, without imposing any conditions, he accepted. But he couldn't move anywhere without taking with him the huge stack of scientific journals that made up his library. There were no books, only journals.

A few years after the end of the War, I finally lost touch with him. Then, to my horror, I heard that—he by now in complete obscurity—his illness had driven him to suicide.

FREDDIE UHLMAN

A very little man, he left his parents in Germany; they were murdered. Originally, he was a barrister in Stuttgart, and worked for "Leftists", and so made a name for himself early in political circles. Since that put him at risk, he went to Paris, decided to become a naive painter, and there, quite by chance, as he said, met Diana, the daughter of a dyed-in-the-wool Conservative father, Sir Henry Page-Croft, who during the Spanish Civil War had spoken out in Parliament for Franco's side, while his daughter was in Paris, working for refugee charities. As a painter and a refugee himself, he paid court to the very young Diana, and, to her father's rage, was accepted. He was summoned to his office and made to stand while he was given a ruthless grilling. A family tree was placed in front of him, with the intention of scaring him off, but he merely found himself favourably impressed by it. "Do you still want to marry my daughter?" came the last question. The tiny Fred Uhlman—but at least he was standing—drew himself up to his full height, said, "Yes, sir," and was shown the door. Freddie loved to rehearse the scene. Diana had inherited the family obstinacy, and even though she was threatened with being cut off, and with future disinheritance a prospect, she stuck to her decision. She wanted to stand by her painter, and help him make his way. They moved into the beautiful old Rossetti House on Downshire

Hill, where William Rossetti, the brother of the painter and poet Dante Gabriel, had lived. On the top floor were refugees from Germany, the most famous of them John Heartfield, who lived there for the duration of the War.

Freddie was a very hard-working painter. He would ask people round to his tasteful studio, where, along with his own pictures, there were better and better quality African statues. Summer parties in his garden were popular affairs, the Hampstead intellectuals liked to meet there, and the occasional émigré. It was possible to hold conversations without being moved on, and you were able to choose for yourself who you talked to. Also, Freddie had a gift for bringing people together—he had an eerily acute sense of every focus of human ambition. By and by, he succeeded in creating a sort of counter-opinion to his father-in-law's, who viewed him as an interloper and a dowry hunter. And so he was able to find people who were interested in his pictures. The link to Paris had been broken by the War, previously Paris had been the be-all and end-all, but for the time being no work of living naive artists— Vivin, Bombois, and the like—could be supplied. Freddie endeavoured to supplant them in London.

A Kulturbund had been started in London before the War, for émigrés from German-speaking countries. Writers, artists and scholars belonged to it. Lectures were given, exhibitions held, English poets who were interested in modern German culture (Stephen Spender, for example) were asked along to give readings. Fred Uhlman was the soul of this Kulturbund, its secretary or perhaps its president (I don't remember), and he was absolutely indefatigable. Oskar Kokoschka was in London, and as he always took part in official events, he could be used as a sort of honorary president, perhaps he was even given such a title, and Freddie Uhlman bandied his name about with great fanfare.

It was a bad time for Kokoschka. No-one knew him in London. German Expressionism had no presence, everything was directed towards France, and Kokoschka's great early period had no significance here. Since his early years in Vienna, his painting had undergone great changes, first in Dresden, then on his subsequent travels. To some people, his portraits seemed to constitute a return to Impressionism. Even his fiftieth-birthday exhibition in Vienna in 1937 had included many portraits that were reminiscent of Liebermann. Whatever you thought of him, he was a great painter, the most significant painter in London at the time—and not only in émigré circles. He was in London with Olda, his magnificently upright wife, completely destitute, and desperate for portrait commissions. There was astonishingly little interest. Official England still clung to the traditional painting of the Royal Academy, whose great days, with the landscapes of Constable and Turner, were long past. Insofar as the graft of French modernism had taken at all, it was confined to a highly cultured, but very small circle of people, and generally more the world of literature than that of painting, which continued to find the separation from France traumatic. For a painter like Kokoschka, there was absolutely no constituency, and it was possible to count the number of commissions that came his way on the fingers of one hand. And so, his name carried huge weight, but only among the émigrés, whereas Freddie Uhlman with his subtlety, and his effective and rather English tactics, managed to sell not a few of his paintings. It took a little time for Kokoschka to understand what was going on, and that his name was just being used, and then he said what he thought about it very clearly in his own way.

Since Kokoschka has come up, probably I should stick with him now. But I can't make myself drop the delicious Freddie, so soon after his own appearance. He is an inexhaustible subject. With his aspirations to nobility—all his life, he ogled anything blue-blooded, but it also needed to be practical—he finally did get somewhere after all. A story from his Stuttgart schooldays about a noble classmate who later sacrificed himself in the July plot against Hitler, written in his last year of life, appeared with a preface by Arthur Koestler, and was filmed after Freddie's death. No-one mentions the paintings now, to which Freddie gave fifty years of his life, but with that little tale, which comes from the profoundest thing in him, his fascination with the nobility, he became known everywhere. It was like that for the whole of the English emigration. Croft Castle, the property of his brother-in-law Michael, who inherited the title from a childless cousin, the castle that he was so proud of that he carried photographs of it around with him wherever he went, showing them to everyone—complete strangers, if they happened to be sitting there—even though he was only very rarely permitted to set foot there, because his Swabian-accented English was an embarrassment to his cousin, after the war. All his incessant business on his own behalf turned out to be in vain, and Freddie attained the fame he was so desperate to achieve via an old classmate whom he idolised as an aristocrat, and who then cut him dead in the Nazi period. That classmate joined the July conspirators, and paid for it with his life.

It was the most remarkable thing that had happened to him in his long life; the Nazis lost the War; German cities, his own birthplace Stuttgart among them, were in ruins; but the school chum who made the deepest impression on him paid for it with his life.

After the innumerable stories I heard from Freddie Uhlman—he never met you without embarking on one—all the desperate, knotted attempts to make himself a witty and interesting raconteur finally left a bitter aftertaste, because, come what may, in all of it you sensed his hatred, hatred for the listener, hatred also for anyone who, in any way, however trivial, had a better time of it than he did.

CE POIDS! CE POIDS!

I dropped in at the Coffee Cup, the Hampstead café that opened after the War. Freddie was sitting there, and beckoned me over to his table. He introduced me to a man with an etched and weathered face, like that of someone who had been on a lot of expeditions and field trips. This was a Parisian art dealer, who was a particular specialist in African art. He had travelled many times through the rich territories of the West of Africa, and brought many fine pieces back to Paris. Freddie had bought some for his own collection, and he admired him for his drive, and wanted to show off to me with him. He quizzed him, so to speak, on my behalf, and got him to speak vividly and interestingly. The dealer was a strong man, with thick, heavy shoulders, well travelled and fearless, and perhaps, after all his adventures and scrapes, just a little blasé. He spoke French, not too showily, and story followed story, peril after peril. He was a little more reticent where business was concerned, as though not wishing to talk about any more favourable circumstances there might be in his life, but he moaned that his sources were drying up, *too many* people had been buying. We came to speak of the painters in Paris. Picasso, of course, he knew and admired, but it wasn't the painting as such that captivated him. He had something Herculean in his head when he spoke of him, and said repeatedly, with his clenched fists raised above his shoulder, as

if raising something with huge exertion: "*Ce poids! Ce poids!*"
His face was contorted by this effort, he said it so often that I
had time to wonder just what it was that Picasso had to carry
around like that. Then the answer came: "Millions! Millions!
Millions!" He said it as often as he had said "*Ce poids!*" before,
and I was no wiser than I was before. What millions was he
talking about? Then things became a little clearer. Picasso was
keeping back a number of paintings, which he didn't want to
sell. Their value was rising and rising, and so he was carrying a
vast fortune on his shoulders, and was using all his strength,
because he knew they were going to be more and more
valuable, the weight was getting heavier and heavier, and I am
unable to think of this art dealer, whose name I will not divulge,
except as a weightlifter, with trembling arms and great beads of
sweat on his face.

On another occasion, Freddie got on to the subject of his
wartime experiences. As the War began, he had found himself
interned, like a number of German and Austrian émigrés, and
had spent six or seven months in a camp on the Isle of Man. He
often told me about some of the distinguished people he had
met while he was there. It was quite astonishing, the people
they had there. But there was one name that never came up,
and it wasn't till some years after the War that Kurt Schwitters
became famous, and his prices went up, and then Freddie duly
came out with him. He was utterly perplexed by the change in
him, he could hardly fathom it, Schwitters had once been such
a wild and temperamental fellow. And now here he was,
keeping himself to himself, sitting hunkered in a corner,
doodling something, unwilling to speak, and not at all eager to
have anyone's attention. In fact, the only reason he had been
noticed at all had been because he had been so retiring. Not
that he had been unpleasant to the others in any way, he had

been as nice as it was possible to be, he looked utterly anonymous, and now: These prices! These prices! When his name was mentioned, one felt Freddie's self-reproach: Why hadn't he bought anything of his at the time? Or maybe Schwitters had even wanted to give him something, and he hadn't paid it any attention, but I'm no longer sure whether that was ever the case or not.

HENRY MOORE AND
ROLAND PENROSE
THE PARTY IN THE BLITZ
THE BATTLE OF BRITAIN
HAMPSTEAD HEATH

In a house further up Downshire Hill, on the other side, Henry Moore had lived for a few years before the War. There was a statue of his in the front garden, which aroused general disfavour, even in this generally enlightened and arty street. He had moved out, and the house was now occupied—at the beginning of the War already—by Roland Penrose, who was a famously wealthy patron of the arts. He had spent much time in Paris, and had lived among the Surrealists, he painted a little in that style himself, but what he did was of no consequence. He had been one of the earliest collectors of Surrealist art, and there were many such paintings to be seen in his house. He knew Picasso well—later on, he wrote a book about him. He lived with an ex-girlfriend of Picasso's, an American photographer by the name of Lee Miller, a strikingly blonde woman with a lascivious expression, who always seemed debauched, perhaps she wasn't really, but she certainly did all she could to create that impression.

It was there, in that house, that I experienced the party in the Blitz. It was some time after the Battle of Britain. In those days of September 1940, you could watch the dogfights between the

British and German planes from up on the Heath, where we were living at the time. In the middle of the day, you could look up at the sky, and watch the tracks of the planes, like watching some sporting event. It was so thrilling that you only had eyes for each particular duel as it was in progress. Perhaps you felt a little proud of the British for performing so well, it was, after all, after Dunkirk. Whereas here, in the air, you got the sense that German planes went down more frequently than British ones. One thought rather less about the consequence of this fighting, we weren't to know what was riding on the outcome. If we had been able to guess that Hitler would abandon his planned invasion of England as a result, we might have been gripped in a different, more strategic way. We were visiting a friend who lived in the Vale of Health, right in the middle of Hampstead Heath, from her first-floor windows you could watch the fighting with extraordinary clarity. It was a particularly beautiful autumn day, the sky was clear and deeply blue, and against it we could see the zigzags of the planes marked in little puffs of white. I won't try to describe what I saw, but I want to try and regain the feeling that gripped me then. I was very excited—I already said, it was like some sporting occasion—but felt utterly innocent, as though it weren't a matter of people's lives and deaths. The planes and the men in them were fused to single beings, a kind of aerial centaur, you could say. What you cared about were the lines . . . They vanished from view, and then they were back, you thought you could make out the planes, which was barely possible to the naked eye, and if you saw that one had been shot down, you didn't think of the fate of the individual man, because up there the shining lines and the great speeds continued. The combination of excitement and dispassion during those hours are to me the most curious part of the memory.

HAMPSTEAD CHURCH ROW
THE CEMETERY

Church Row was a little street of Georgian houses. It was, with the odd exception, almost in its original condition. At the far end of it stood Hampstead Parish Church, which had been restored in 1745. The cemetery around the church was older than that, some of the graves in it dated back to the seventeenth century. These old cemeteries, which are never very big, are some of the most attractive features of the English landscape. You find them in older settlements, in the Chilterns for example, where industrialisation hasn't wrecked everything: Hampstead was once a little spa on a hill north of London. In the eighteenth century, there was a fad for going there to take the waters. A number of the most famous writers and painters in the country met in Hampstead. The painters came for the landscape of Hampstead Heath, and one of the greatest English painters, John Constable, is buried in Hampstead cemetery. His gravestone is visited by people from all over the world, many have come to the cemetery just to see it. I too have paid him my respects, but it wasn't for his sake that I went to the cemetery all those years of my time in Hampstead. First, you passed a few yew trees (the trees whose wood furnished the bows at Agincourt), and then you lost your way among upright and moss-grown tombstones. They were tough granite, and had withstood the test of time; most of the inscriptions were still legible, and they weren't in the dismal barracks-like order of more modern cemeteries. There was something individual about a lot of these stones, even in their posture. Some seemed always to have been standing slightly askew, while with others the soil below must have shifted. The slight differentiations in the humus on this hill added to the variety. Each stone had acquired some special characteristic, through time, through its angle, through its position in relation to the crooked paths. There were no curves, nothing that had the appearance of geometry, or perhaps there was some unresearched cemetery geometry, but one that didn't lend itself to human exploration. One thing, though, was exposed to any passing look: the dates on the stones. Sometimes, not often, they were blurred, but they never changed, they were, so to speak the backbone of the cemetery; it was here and from them that I learned what cemeteries are, and if I may once have expressed it too bluntly and categorically, I should like to offer a correction to that now at this late stage in my life. It was unavoidable that one felt superior to the possessor of the grave by the number of years that had passed since its erection, as if one had been so many years older, merely because the stone offered itself to be looked at, but this wasn't a *hard* feeling, it was, if anything, a peaceable feeling, one that was shared in some way with the denizen of the grave. Because the fact that one was able to stand there and contemplate the passing of so much time also did him credit: you read his name, you perhaps spoke it half-aloud to yourself, you had no reason to bear him any ill will, and if you didn't feel gratitude to him as such, you did, in a simple, natural way let him participate in the time in which you were contemplating him. It may sound strange, but it helps to explain the warm feeling you had, when you came up to some of these stones, and gazed at them, as if you had known

Elias Canetti in the cemetery, Church Row, Hampstead Heath

the people. Sometimes, this may seem hard to credit, I felt
something approaching curiosity towards the subject of the
inscription. Why was it you came back, why did you return so
often, what caused you to stop, not every time, but often? The
names and dates had etched themselves into you, and who is to
say how many of the dead kept their names for you? I still carry
their names in my head. It would be silly to list them here, with
their dates, but it is a fact that, while I have forgotten many
things—and forget more with every day that passes—these
names are marked in my head as much as they are on the stone.

Hampstead consists for me of those people I knew there, of
those who were famous as artists in their time, and who still are,
and of those whose names I learned from their stones.

It was like the discharging of a debt that no-one can repay,
when I went there. I felt somehow lighter, and more righteous

than I did in day-to-day life. Only later, and infrequently, did I go there with people I liked, and whom I wanted to give a feeling of something that was indispensable to me. When I went there on my own, I didn't feel sorrow, but the question, in its immutable reality: How did they take to it, this thing to which there is no answer, and how will we take to it in our time? Is it the inscribed stones that keep us asking the question? And if you felt a fondness for the stones, because their people are not present—is that such an inexplicable feeling? I don't mind saying so much, because seeing as I have failed to find the answer myself, I want to preserve the question in its full force.

THE PARTY AT PENROSE'S
THE FIREMEN

I have mentioned Roland Penrose and Lee Miller, his girlfriend. They were obsessed by Paris, and represented the currently fashionable aspect of art. There was something a little mean about him, perhaps it came from his puritan background. Apparently he came from an old Quaker family. A lot of the people I most respected, during the War too, had a stubborn dedication in themselves, but the object of this dedication had changed in him, and the fame of Picasso, to whom he now consecrated himself, was liable to engulf people who did not themselves have a comparable luminosity. Penrose served him by buying his paintings. That was, even then, not a rare art, but he served too the Surrealists, whose paintings he also bought, and while London was cut off from Paris, he became something like their English centre. I do not know how he really felt about the War, in the externals of his life, he seemed to be quite unaffected by it.

When the Blitzkrieg began over London, a few months after Dunkirk, in the most dangerous period of English history, I attended a party at his house, which would remain vividly present to me, even if I were to live another 500 years. His house was higher than most of those on Downshire Hill. It had three floors, most of the others just had two. It was no wider or deeper than most of the others. Each floor consisted of just one room or two at the most. They were full of people, drinking and dancing. They stood around, glass in hand, as was the way here, but with expressive faces, which was rather irregular. Among them were some young officers in uniform, lively, almost animated, bubbling up with loud sentences, which one would have heard if the music had been any quieter. The dancers, the women especially, had something lascivious about them, and they relished their own movements, as well as those of their partners. The atmosphere was thick and warm, and no-one seemed to be concerned that we could hear bombs coming down, it was a fearless and a very lively group. I had started out on the top floor, I could hardly believe my eyes, then I walked down to the second floor, and believed them still less. Each room seemed more fiery than the one I had been in before. In the lower rooms, people sought a little privacy for themselves, couples sat embracing, the music pushed through us hotly, from top to bottom, people were hugging and kissing, nothing seemed indecent, in the basement, there were the most astounding goings-on. The door into the garden was ajar, men in firemen's helmets reached for buckets of sand, which they carried out very fast, with sweat on their faces. They heeded nothing they saw in the room, in their haste to protect the burning houses in the neighbourhood, they reached blindly for the sand-filled buckets. There must have been any number of them, the couples, not quite so many down here, continued to hold each other hard, no-one let go of his or her partner, it was as though the panting, sweating labourers had nothing whatever to do with them, they were two different species, each oblivious to the other, that's how it seemed, but the appearance was deceptive, because that evening the fire brigade consisted of volunteers from the same street, including the odd young poet, whom I would never have recognised in his exertions.

I must add that the air attacks at this time were not what they later became (say, on German cities, some of which were obliterated), it was something whose terror consisted largely of its unfamiliarity.

After about an hour, I left the house, I was neither frightened nor indignant, though I was embarrassed by the unflappable lovers beside the puffing firemen; but as the latter showed not the least surprise, merely plunging in and out again, they didn't try to bust anything up; leaving the others undisturbed seemed to be at least as important to them as it did to the lovers that they remained entwined. On each side there was determination, I was amazed by the self-control of the English, who refused to be distracted by anything or anyone, then I was embarrassed by my own embarrassment, and thought I felt what English Puritanism really was, which I had always been frightened and in awe of.

Diagonally across the road was No. 35, the house that contained the geometrical-abstract collection of Margaret Gardiner. Roland Penrose's house had the Surrealists, their antithesis. Neither the one nor the other scorned or oppressed. Above and to the side, the War, England at any moment expecting an invasion, its first in 900 years. Not the least inclination, before the invasion, to give anything up on account of it, the only ones to fear the worst the émigrés. The English themselves so calm that I could not help but gawp at times in disbelief. The party wasn't the only time I was reduced to such amazement.

THE FREEMASONS ARMS
FRIEDL

At the bottom of Downshire Hill, opposite No. 35, the house where I used to come and go, was a . . . pub, quite a big pub, you could eat lunch in the back room, in the front room was the bar, on the inside the usual games and machines, a terrace at the side, that didn't get too packed, even when the weather was fine, giving on to a large garden. At certain times, people with glasses would be standing outside the pub, but it never seemed intrusive, the important things were always going on inside, the famed English standing-up conversations, which here were less formulaic than was usually the case, because the local people were largely artists and intellectuals. The people you saw in this pub were mostly already known, there weren't many tyros, and those there were at least already had their protectors and didn't stand there completely stranded. Friedl and her cousin, the collector Margaret Gardiner who lived over the road, used to drop in all the time, and if ever they didn't feel like going—it was perhaps too familiar to them—then they could always see out of their own windows who was going in, who was going out, who stood around for a while, there was no other entrance, the people at No. 35 kept tabs on everything.

When I called round sometimes, Friedl or Margaret would take me over the road, and introduce me to this person or that, who had been known there for ages, who hadn't been seen for decades, who had resurfaced just a year ago. Usually they were people whose names were associated with someone of great fame, for having discovered them, loved them, or upset them. A little old plump man with red cheeks and a wily, innocent face, who looked as though he couldn't count up to three, drank a lot, and winked, as though he would have liked to get the better of you, who was always there, before the War, during, and even for some time after, was Mr Roberts, who long ago had been a publisher, and had led Joyce a dance for years over his first book, *Dubliners*. He had accepted it, and then not accepted it, he had complaints and suggestions, he had cut some things and wanted others reinstated, and then didn't. Joyce talked about it all, and the details are known, but no longer to me. What couldn't be forgiven was the depth of the disappointment he caused Joyce, the extent of the suffering— perhaps that was even the spur that kept him away from the British Isles for the remainder of his life, once he'd left Dublin. At the time, it wasn't that one would have hated the fellow for it, it was more of a quirky story that he was still around. Imagine how it would be today, where Joyce is being delved into and investigated down to the smallest detail. Anyway, there he was, standing there, perfectly ordinary and a little boring, conducting dull conversations with people on either side of him, I would have heard enough to have put me off for a lifetime, if I hadn't also happened to have heard: This is the man whom James Joyce hated more than any other.

But how unfair, to mention only this one of so many, there are innumerable people one no longer thinks about, just because they aren't frying in James Joyce's private hell.

FRIEDL'S GENEROSITY
THE BLOUSE
STEVIE SMITH

Friedl, who brought me here, had something to say about everyone, some of it I was already familiar with from the diaries she kept for me. People instinctively trusted her, no-one noticed the way she took possession of everything with her green eyes, and then wrote it down verbatim as she'd learned to do (as I had told her to do). As soon as she'd filled up a notebook, she passed it to me, not least as proof of her rather doubtful diligence. But she went on doing this, even after she'd embarked on her novels, which she began in German, and, with the help of the diaries, completed in English.

She got to meet countless people, and was well liked by all. "*Ici vient la jeunesse!*" exclaimed an admiring Belgian painter and fearless art dealer, seeing her come up or down Downshire Hill. Her much older cousin Margaret soon learned to draw profit from her attractiveness. Her own charms were fading, but she needed to remain attractive, and this she was able to do with Friedl at her side. Numbers of guests were invited, the house had always been on the map for artists, and with the collection that was kept there, all abstract, it struck its own inimitable note.

Unlike her cousin, Friedl had no property, but she was of a

boundless generosity. When Stevie Smith, a witty, original, wholly unsentimental poetess once came to lunch, to meet Friedl, she admired the white silk blouse she had on for the first time, and told her so in her characteristically blunt fashion. Friedl excused herself, left the room, and came back a few moments later, with the white blouse in her hands, and held it out to Stevie: "It's yours," and it all sounded so natural, as though she couldn't possibly keep such a beautiful thing, not if Stevie Smith—a typically English old maid, a picture of ugliness—happened to like it. But the old maid was a poetess, her bluntness was bracing, she derived her style of writing from nonsense verse, and had rightly become famous round about this time. Overwhelmed she kept the blouse, which she would have never dared to wear, just to refresh the memory of such generosity by looking at it, and she went on to talk about Friedl everywhere she went. When she saw the blouse, generosity welled up in her, which otherwise she would not, with her ugliness, have been capable of. She had the feeling then of swimming in it, and she admired Friedl, the body of water that had so much of it.

One aspect of Friedl's magnanimity was the stupefying disorder in which she lived. As long as she was staying at her cousin's, it wasn't too obvious, the coloured squares of Ben Nicholson's on almost every wall—derived from Mondrian—created their own fiction of order. But as soon as she was living on her own, at the end of the War, she was submerged in chaos—a dreadful collapse.

OSKAR KOKOSCHKA

O K., as he was called by his Czech wife Olda, a tall young woman, with a beautiful horsey face, that was somewhat reminiscent of some of Michelangelo's faces. Oskar Kokoschka lived in London during the war years, barely noticed by the English public. A quiet man, so quiet you often couldn't understand what he was saying. His German, still unmistakably moulded by Vienna, in spite of all his subsequent travels, the tone, if audible, fluidly intense. He was all alone when he came to London, except for Olda, whom he had first met when she was six in her parents' house in Prague, he had gone down on his knees for her, had gone up to her as a child seemingly not much older than herself, and said: "You're my bride. I'm going to marry you." She never forgot, grew up, became a student, and when one day he came to Prague again from Dresden, an emigrant now, and a "degenerate artist", to paint the portrait of President Masaryk, he saw her again, she remained with him, and accompanied him into further emigration, to London. There she was, the svelte giantess, always in attendance on him, without ever making the least fuss on her own account, listening to him respectfully but never ingratiatingly as he spoke to visitors, adjusting to the arabesque style of his talk, full of leaps and parentheses, and in its chaotic way containing some profoundly original remarks and observations. I once happened to witness the way misunderstandings produced ideas for him so directly, that I will relate it in all its absurd triviality. A visitor—I was there too, silent, as I usually was when in his company, you couldn't have a conversation with him, he would always be talking, and it was so hard to hear him that you had no energy left for any quick replies—a visitor, then, was just explaining to him why he, the visitor, smoked. It wasn't that he especially liked the taste, nor the oral craving, it was purely and simply pleasure in having money go up in smoke. Kokoschka, who was just then smoking a cigarette himself, paused, kept his cigarette in his mouth a little longer than usual, took it between his fingers, rubbed his lips together, and said: "I taste it, the honey." Instead of "money", he had heard "honey", had tested out the other fellow's putative remark on the spot, and it seemed so unexpected to him that it was true. The misunderstanding was subsequently explained, but he didn't like that, he had had the taste of honey on his lips after inhaling the smoke, and that was how it remained. In a less extreme way, this was how all conversations were with him: he only listened in order to hear something eccentric, something told him by his own senses. What someone said to him either had no effect at all, as though it hadn't been heard, as though nobody had heard it, or seemed to be something that Kokoschka either had always known or had just this minute learned. His continuous assimilation of the external world was not always so innocent. It might also have intent—the use of people for particular purposes, for intrigues and calculations—but it remained such a curious process, a tissue of seemingly superfluous things, and something so essential to him that you wouldn't use the word calculation for it.

His zigzag speeches always contained some germ of reminiscence in the way that poets have; perhaps they were even more concrete; affection and annoyance, injury, pride in independence, such a mighty show of being swayed, that it came down to a wild impossibility of being swayed. He hated anything abstract in art. He rejected Cubism, and certainly all of Picasso, who had once spoken slightingly of a painting of his in his Paris show. Some of his contemporaries from the early years in Vienna he was at pains to erase from human memory. Schiele amounted to nothing on his own, he had been in Kokoschka's studio, and stolen from him the things that later made him famous. To Loos he remained grateful, his name had a fixed sound when he said it, as if it were some unassailable piece of gold currency, but he never told any exaggerated or overly personal stories about him. His gratitude took the form of discretion. Nor would he use him for any of his plots. For otherwise, he wove everyone together. He was capable of making a network of people, even if he had only just heard their names. And these new formations went on being woven, and some turned into his favourite stories, with which he regaled everyone.

At the beginning of the War, when I saw him again—two or three years after our first meeting in Prague—I hadn't been with him for more than half an hour when he made me his monstrous confession. He was to blame for the War, in that Hitler, who had wanted to be a painter, had been driven into politics. Oskar Kokoschka and Hitler were both applying for the same scholarship from the Viennese Academy. Kokoschka was successful, Hitler turned down. If Hitler had been accepted instead of Kokoschka, Kokoschka would never have wound up in politics, there would have been no National Socialist Party, and no Second World War. In this way, Kokoschka was to blame for the War. He said it almost beseechingly, with far more emphasis than he usually had, and he repeated it several times, in a conversation that had moved on to other matters, he brought it back, and I had the dismaying impression that he was putting himself in Hitler's place. Only it was incontestably true that he did not even share a tenth of an opinion with Hitler, he was, with undiminished resolve, against everything he stood for, he hated racism, he loathed war, the fact that his painting had been classed as "degenerate" had hurt him deeply. But it was impossible for him to be implicated in history without having some *significance*, even if it were guilt, a rather dubious guilt at that. He hated to be without influence, and he tried to use every one of the handful of people he knew at that time for his own purposes, among them political purposes.

I witnessed a frivolous example of this when he met Veza. She had never yet failed to impress a painter, she was beautiful even in the reduced circumstances in which we were living at the time. He turned to her immediately with the astonishing remark that one had to make the most of whatever influence one might have on this war, it was important, it was a duty. I was baffled by his words, I couldn't understand them, and Veza understood them still less, till he suddenly mentioned the name Hore-Belisha.

Hore-Belisha was a short-lived War Minister — then still just in office—who was very distantly related to Veza. His uncle was married to Veza's cousin, a younger namesake, who was called "little Veza" in the family. The two Vezas had a sort of crush on one another, and had written each other letters from girlhood. Now, "big" Veza had never met Hore-Belisha, but had heard a lot about him, as she told me. I had once mentioned that in a conversation with Kokoschka, months ago, never repeated it, and explained quite plainly that Veza had never met the man. He had remembered this, and raised it with her the first time they met, telling her to use her *influence* and to *advise* him, although first she would have to make his acquaintance, that was now her number-one priority. When she had got her bearings—she was given time to do so, because Kokoschka harped on and on about this—she said: "But how can I advise him? I don't know the first thing about it!" She meant munitions and materiel, and was just wanting to say something in her confusion. Her disappointment and bewilderment were great, she had expected a lot from Kokoschka. She was familiar with his name from early girlhood, when his first pictures caused a stir and something of a scandal in Vienna. Now here he was, talking incessantly about this War Minister, whom she thought of as insignificant, and whose name he stumbled over in his bad English. She was accustomed to being complimented by painters; from Kokoschka, the most famous painter she had ever met, she hadn't expected any, but she was at least looking for original remarks on paintings and writers. When, in her fiery way she decided on a change of subject, and asked him what he thought of Peter Altenberg, he winked at her, it was his way of indicating a rejection—although he could also wink to show he agreed—he levelled his . . . octopus eye on her again, took her in without really paying any attention to her, and said one last time: "Hore-Belisha, don't forget, it's important!"

Maybe he would have liked to paint her, he had very few portrait commissions at that time. But, while that might have crossed his mind, what he really cared about was the prospect of having influence on higher circles. I was still inclined at that time, I was thirty-four years old, to take great artists for saints, no questions asked, and why should he be any different?

Later on, Veza got to know him better as well. Another relic of his life had been entrusted to us by Anna Mahler when we moved out to the country. This was the famous set of six fans painted on swan-parchment for Alma Mahler, and presented to her. After she had moved to America, she had left them with her daughter in London; at that time, she really didn't give very much for that poor émigré Kokoschka, who had been strikingly poor even at the time of their passionate affair. But you never knew, times changed, and maybe they would one day be valuable. So she left them with Anna, who had true respect for great artists, and took good care of them. The Blitz came, houses went up in flames, paintings were burned to cinders, she was determined to stay in London, but when Veza, her trusted friend, and I moved out to the country, she asked us to take the fans with us, and look after them.

We had already been living a few weeks in Amersham, or more precisely in Chesham Bois, when Kokoschka heard that his fans, which he hadn't seen for twenty years, were with us. He came to see us, to see them again, and the hour he sat with us with the fans in his hands, and told us their story, was the most gripping I ever spent with him.

He sat in a corner, Veza and I either side of him. He took up the fans in order, and evoking his early graphic and colouristic work in words, he moved in a way I had never yet seen a man move. Everything happened a second time, or (this really happened) it seemed more real to me than on the fans (which Veza and I had already admired by ourselves). He did not seek to reclaim the gift of the fans. Nor did he say anything about the fact that the woman they had been for had not taken them with her, but left them with Gucki. That was her daughter, Anna, a little child cowering in his atelier, watching the extraordinary outbursts of his jealous rage against her mother from the very beginning. It wasn't at all against the order of things that the fans should be with the daughter. She was the third person there, and she retained a profound aversion to "scenes", which later on—dispassionately, unlike her mother—she was to provoke in her own life. Kokoschka said nothing about her now, her work didn't interest him. He never visited her, perhaps he would not have gone to see the fans in her keeping, even if he had discovered she had them. With us, he could see them, and go into his displays of excitement, which we paid him the compliment of taking seriously. I had read a lot about shamans at that time, especially accounts of them in Siberia. As we experienced the visions being created out of his fans, I felt what a shaman really is. All the cunning that forms part of it, and the "political" instinct, so developed with him, were there, and his vehemence, which had bothered and disturbed me, suddenly seemed perfectly natural to me.

I suppose, after talking about these fans so much, I should describe them, but I won't. Everyone knows about them. Ever since the exhibition in the Städel devoted to Kokoschka and his life-sized doll, the newspapers have been full of these fans, there have been numerous depictions of them, anyone who wants to can see them, whoever feels so unsettled by them that he has to see them can go to Frankfurt and visit them in the Städel.

IRIS MURDOCH

Yesterday, the thick philosophical tome by Iris Murdoch, with her name on the cover in huge letters. I—unfortunately—sat down with it for a few hours. My antipathy against her has grown so strong that I must say something about her here.

Her book is very badly written, sloppily, like lectures that haven't been revised sufficiently. The tone is academic in the worst way. It wouldn't matter so much if she had something to say, but all she does is quote hundreds of passages and pronouncements of Wittgenstein, in that slavish way of the Wittgenstein cult, particularly in Oxford. On top of that there is the cult of the past couple of decades: Derrida, much earlier it used to be Sartre, on whom she wrote a little booklet, her first. Freud is of course there as if he'd never been away, he's a cult of the century. Then Heidegger, who took over from Hegel with her once upon a time. She talks about Marxism, as if it were something that predated her, not without respect, but with an indescribable display of boredom. I don't think there is anything that leaves me quite so cold as that woman's intellect. She is a passionate schoolgirl, of the kind that likes nothing better than studying systems. She seems to realise herself in that compulsion. And then she's the schoolmarm who likes to *explain* these systems. Of course, she's desperate to avoid any misrepresentations. So she faithfully reproduces everything, it won't be distorted that way—in her thinking she resembles nothing less than a poetess—and then there's the next system, equally undistorted in its transmission and as a kind of school subject. She's over seventy, so she has a wonderful collection of systems. The whole thing is topped off with morality, she is passionate—if one can use the word in the context of this mumbo-jumbo—in the way she sticks up for traditional morality.

She also has something quite different to stick up for: and those are her twenty-four novels. These contain all the Oxford gossip she has heard in half a century. All her characters are Oxford born and bred. That means a lot of culture, but for her that culture comes with faces attached. In her time she has been in love with innumerable men (not to mention many women), but they were *special* men, each of them a specialist in his own chosen field, whom she took up with. There really were all sorts: a theologian, an economist, an ancient historian, a literary critic, an anthropologist, and also a philosopher and a writer.

The relationship I know most about is the one with the writer, which is me. The literary critic (and historian) is her husband, John Bayley, with whom she has lived these past forty years. The two of them have endless discussions about literature, it's something he knows much more about than she does, his opinions are a little more distinctive, he's less chaotic. But all these men she has taken into her, they're all metamorphoses of herself. Her characters spring from the endless discussions she's had with all these men. The women are herself, her woman friends and her girl students, but everything comes out of that Oxford air, in which, thanks to her readiness to love, she has moved and remained with astonishing ease. One might think of admiring it, but there is nothing admirable there. She has not one serious thought, everything continues to sleep. You are reminded of the facile transformations of delirium tremens, only with her everything is ordered and made harmless.

True terror she avoids. She knows it only from books. She keeps everything she hears, and—provided it didn't have prior expression as philosophy—it becomes her anonymous booty. I might say she has made a lot of booty from me, but it is mixed with so much other prey, that I'd feel ashamed: it's really more of a liability. The facile plausibility of her books, which are often amusing, is predicated on her way of never telling any stories aloud. There she is either stingy or else she is a gushing philosophy mistress. She listens to everything, again and again, as long as people can stand to repeat it, she offers herself in exchange for more, calmly listens to stories, confessions, ideas, despair. She strikes me as being like a housewife on a shopping expedition. She forgets nothing, you live on in her in a light, irresponsible way, because only philosophy is responsible, and ethics. She also takes on board religions, cumulatively, if you like, never out of any despair of her own, she has her suppliers. Simone Weil is quoted with as much respect as Wittgenstein or Plato.

Plato is the antique kernel of her quoting. It's clear why, he happens in dialogue form, which is to her the air she breathes. He too has become one of her "stimuli". In the last few years, she has composed a few Platonic dialogues.

You could call Iris Murdoch the bubbling Oxford stewpot. Everything I despise about English life is in her. You could imagine her speaking incessantly, as a tutor, and incessantly *listening*: in the pub, in bed, in conversation with her male or female lovers.

She never *completely* adopts anything, just as she never *completely* rejects it, it is all left in a harmless, tolerable, un-worked-out suspension.

Iris Murdoch

Her relationship to art: she travels and goes to museums a lot, she gets hot under the collar, because she's forever talking in front of pictures, or rather: getting others to talk.

Her origins are utterly petit bourgeois. She had a charming Irish mother, who looked more like a sister, prettier than her, more natural, merrier, who married a much older man, a civil servant, who had eyes for nothing but books, who spent all his lunch breaks in the second-hand bookshops on the Charing Cross Road, a tall, dark, contemplative, and very attractive Englishman. That their union produced one child might have been auspicious. (That this child became a vulgar success that swept the nation is something one would have preferred not to predict.)

My chief trait, much my strongest quality, which has never been compromised, was the insistence on myself, not at anyone else's expense, but just so: it was always there for me, and saw me through everything. It may be a sort of virtue, and so it appears to me when I look at Iris's philosophical book. I will never seriously read it. I can't take her seriously any more. That's to do with the fact that I've known her so well. I know how she *came about*, she *assembled herself* practically before my eyes, a kind of all-in-one parasite from Oxford, itself an— attractive—excrescence of humanity. Iris never got Oxford out of her system. Her life is made up of the sort of conversations that are typical of that place, either she listens to them or she writes them down. I will now do for once what she *always* does: I will describe her, describe Iris.

Iris Murdoch: I was struck by her way of listening, the very first time I saw her with Franz Steiner. She was listening like a deaf person, who, to hear at all, tries to soak up everything. Her face was Flemish, like an early Memling. It often and easily crumpled up into a tearful expression, but she didn't cry. Just at the point of tears, she stopped, although the crying face held out a while longer. I ascribed to her a much longer, profounder loyalty than she actually felt, because after Steiner's death, for which she felt partly responsible, she would often come to me, to rail at herself. She was mourning Steiner, but she kept a sharp eye on me, to see whether, in offering her comfort, I would try to make an approach to her.

She was supposed to go back to Oxford, it was getting late, it was foggy, I asked her if she wanted to stay the night. She could lock herself into the room where we were presently sitting, I would sleep somewhere else. I said this out of respect for her grief, she wasn't to suppose for a moment that I was trying to make an approach to her, not when she'd spent hour after hour talking about Steiner. Her face, which had the tearful expression the whole time, but without crying, won me for her. On account of her suffering, I took her so seriously that I wanted to free her of any stirrings of possible suspicion of me. She looked at me with a doubtful expression, I thought it might be uncertainty, but actually it was surprise and disappointment. She didn't take up my offer, and went back to Oxford, I walked her as far as the Finchley Road tube station, went down the steps with her, and left her sitting on a bench with the book in her hand I had just given her: *The Lyrebird*, an account of a woman's friendship with one such bird in the Australian desert, it danced and sang for her. This magical book, which I had only recently discovered myself, I gave her, she understood the significance of it, it was a sort of baptism, which indicated that she was accepted among the writers. At that time, there were no books by her (it was early 1953, now she has twenty-four novels alone). I left her in the fog, waiting for her train, at that time we weren't so close that I would have waited with her. I vanished up the steps, the fog was very thick, I looked back and couldn't see anything, the fog had swallowed her up, I thought of her pain-filled face, and felt concerned for her, I stopped and went back down the stairs, and suddenly stood in front of her; she was sitting on the bench, happily leafing through the book I had given her. Her face of sorrow had become a beam of happiness, touched with light amazement at this book. And what writer wouldn't have been amazed by this bird, which was itself a poet.

I felt then for the first time that her grief wasn't all there was of her, that I had succeeded in freeing her of her painful guilt. That was why she had come, that was why I made her welcome. To me it was as though I owed it to Steiner to free her from her torment.

The train came, she got up, and in a trice she had disappeared into the fog, doubly disappeared. I walked back to my flat in a state of some confusion, and was happy, happy at the thought of her happy face looking at the book.

She visited again in the course of that winter, she was always talking about Steiner, and we kissed. I don't remember when exactly it happened, but it happened very soon, and it was the familiar pained face. I have to say it is not common in England to make a display of pain, most reasonably well-brought-up people keep their faces expressionless, and one doesn't see that there is anything going on in the person beneath.

But the extraordinary thing happened as soon as we had kissed. The couch I always slept on was to hand. Quickly, very quickly, Iris undressed, without me laying a finger on her, she had things on that didn't have anything remotely to do with love, it was all woollen and ungainly, but in no time it was in a heap on the floor, and she was under the blanket on the couch. There wasn't time to look at her things or herself. She lay unmoving and unchanged, I barely felt myself enter her, I didn't sense that she felt anything, perhaps I might have felt something if she had resisted in some form. But that was as much out of the question as any pleasure. The only thing I noticed was that her eyes darkened, and that her reddish Flemish skin got a little redder.

No sooner was it finished, she was still lying flat on her back, than she became animated and started to talk. She was caught in a peculiar dream: she was in a cave with me, I was a pirate, I had snatched her away and dragged her back to my cave, where I had flung her down and ravished her. I sensed how happy she was with this pretty commonplace story, she got a little redder still, and felt hot to the touch. She wanted to see me as a brigand, who brutally forced her, she only got excited when she was able to imagine herself with the corsair from the East. I tried to tell myself it had been my account of my childhood in the Balkans, then still under Turkish suzerainty, that had prompted this fantasy of an attack by pirates.

I didn't show her how amused I was. Any way to loving her was blocked off by this dream. It would be impossible to imagine anything further from my mind than this ravishing. Perhaps, if things had happened very differently, I might have been able to love her.

As it was, though, it remained an embarrassingly one-sided story, which I accepted against my better judgement, and observed dispassionately. I had letters from her, very passionate, which I never answered. (From time to time she would turn up herself and expect love—in short order—but she always remained impassive, and afterwards slipped into her little fantasy again.) Once, it was in the form of a very long poem, which she wrote out for me, it didn't have the least thing to do with me, even though—I say this sheepishly, and without any pride—it was intended as a love poem to me. But her inevitable dreams did not have the least distinctiveness, she was only telling me—something I didn't understand till much later—that she wanted to see herself as the pirate. She had a—buried—robber's nature, and her aim was to rob each one of her lovers not of his heart, but more of his mind.

She also had an astonishing relationship with time. She had divided it all up, to her it was like a teacher's timetable. When she called, she would say she was coming at 3.15, and would have to leave at 4.15. It might be a little longer, but it was always constrained, and always set in advance by her how much time she had free, and even though it was about what she termed love, never would she have allowed herself to take more than the allotted time for it. I teased her for this, but, whereas she listened to every syllable from me, she seemed never to understand my contempt for her version of love as an item on her timetable. This went on—with lengthening intervals—for a couple of years. She invited me to Oxford, and met me at the station. She was wearing grotesque sandals, which showed off her large flat feet to terrible disadvantage. I could not ignore the ugliness of her feet. She had a bearlike walk, but it was a repulsive bear, crooked and purposeful at once. Her upper body was delicate and well-proportioned, and the face at moments—including some sexual moments—as beautiful as that of a Memling Madonna. She walked with me from the station into town, pushing a bicycle with one hand, stopped at a dingy shop to buy some wretched provisions—ends of cheese, bread, not even any olives—for lunch, and set it in front of me in the little flat where she was staying. Anything less hospitable, more dismally puritanical, more tasteless than such a meal is impossible to imagine. What was supposed to be the frugal ways of a young scholar was in reality mean and petty bourgeois; the seductiveness of a woman asking one to take a meal was altogether beyond her.

Afterwards she made it clear that there was a couch handy, and she laid herself down on it pretty promptly. While her lack of hospitality may have chilled me, her love never did, for the simple reason that it wasn't love, it was an indifferent act, endowed with a baffling significance for her. I wondered: Was I still her pirate when the setting was Oxford?

She preferred to come to London, because Oxford, where

everyone knew her, and where there were a lot of complicated friendships and enmities, was often difficult for her. I liked Oxford. I had been there with Friedl, who was no longer alive now, and kept a warm feeling for it from that time. Iris knew Friedl's books and admired them. As I talked to her a lot, was open and unreserved—she was generally, and greedily, silent— she was moved by my grief over Friedl. Our relationship was put together from two griefs—hers over Franz Steiner, and mine over Friedl.

(This is the only time in my life that I was with a woman who didn't seek to hold me to her.) For a long time, Iris accepted that I didn't answer her letters. But when she came, I talked to her, passionately excited, about Veza, about Friedl, about others, about all sorts of things. I *liked* having Iris as a listener. I sensed she was good at it, and thought that was what she came to me for. Nothing draws me to a person more than the feeling that they want to listen to me. With Iris, that desire was a passion. I liked her for it. I talked to her about things that meant a lot to me, and she took it all in, almost as intensely as Friedl, though not as hopelessly, because Iris listened to a *lot* of people in the same way (and gave herself to them, in return). She was so insatiable that she got herself embroiled in difficult and complicated affairs. I soon sensed whether a name mattered to her, first—a curiosity—she would speak about people who had been important to her, but then she came out with those she thought she possessed at the time, and who reacted to her escapades with a jealousy to which they thought they were entitled. In reality, they were all escapades, no-one was there *on his own*: perhaps once, a long time ago, but even that seems unlikely to me. Her thirst for knowledge was great, the friends she had in Oxford were generally specialists in this thing or that, there were some very gifted people among them from whom she learned everything one might learn in the course of a love affair. She would never trade anyone in for anyone else, and that got her into a lot of trouble. It was impossible for her to renounce. She crossed women who thought they had a right to certain men, by being married to them, say, and who confronted Iris with a dogged sense of ownership, or with deep-seated malice. That led to terrible humiliations, which she never forgave and which she never talked about either. But there were whole postal districts in London from which she felt herself banished by the wife of some lover or other. It took a new and significant lover to re-animate these places for her, to enable her to move in them with any of her old freedom.

Following this rehearsal of not terribly attractive qualities, it is only fair to say that Iris was in her way very grateful to those whose minds she ransacked, and even over many years never forgot anyone who had once been kind to her. It was with her that I first saw that there could be such a thing as a sense of loyalty to *many people*—perhaps more than anyone can know or count—and saw that that could be as binding as the tie of a loving marriage. In her feelings for *them all* Iris was like an authoress. She never forgot anyone she thought she understood, and even after forty years, she didn't forget to speak of someone like Franz Steiner, for example, as if he had been the one great love of her life.

I continue with what I wrote several days ago about Iris Murdoch, not that it interests me any more, but I should bring it to some sort of conclusion.

Iris is what I would call an "illegitimate" writer. She never suffered from having to write. There was always something schoolgirl-like about her, even after twenty-four novels, and if not schoolgirl-like, then schoolmarmish, which in a writer is even worse.

I think back to the time with Friedl, when I took on the role of a teacher. I was strict with Friedl, in our "proper" time together, I didn't write her any letters. There was nothing resembling "equality" between us. What she wrote—whatever I might think about it now, it's decades since I last read it—was genuine, inasmuch as she allowed herself to be pushed and driven, and was never afraid of any terrible consequences.

Iris always had a regard to everything that might be good for her. In spite of all the chaos and the infractions of her life, she could never completely lose herself. Academe preserved her. She was steeped in the institution of old English universities, especially Oxford. Within that institution, she grazed or nibbled at every person within reach, and everyone outside, so long as there wasn't a danger that he might tear her away. If I think about it now, she was always calculating. There's one example of this that irritated me at the time, almost forty years ago. I told her everything. She got to hear about all the people I knew, and also a good many of those I had known. It's true, she took it all in. She wanted to hear everything I had to say, not just about people who were presently something in my life. But I never (at the time) understood in what spirit she listened to me talking about my current friends.

I was seeing a lot of Aymer at the time. He really interested me; apart from my brother, I had never come across anyone so exclusively interested in young people. He belonged to the very highest ranks of society, that I'd only encountered through him, and in London. His mother was a Percy, the daughter of one of the Dukes of Northumberland. I mocked the significance this seemed to have for many people (among them Kathleen Raine). She was stubbornly in pursuit of Gavin,

Aymer's brother, who was similarly homosexual. But Kathleen was not at all ashamed of showing her social rapacity, her snobbishness. She *adored* people—if they were Percys. She had an indescribable, or rather a disgraceful contempt for people of her own class (or rather, of her father's).

Of Iris I knew that she had long been a Communist; in the period after the War, when it had been possible to go to the Continent again, she had done things of a *conspiratorial* character (I never knew quite what they were). So, when I told her about Aymer, I never supposed for a moment that his society could be anything to her, but somehow she seemed—from what I told her—to get interested and she must have signalled to me that she would like to meet him. She had just become known, following the publication of her first novel *Under the Net*, and Aymer was always curious about literary people. So, on one occasion when we were supposed to have dinner together, with Jean-Max, who was over from Paris, in Hampton Court, and, at my request, Aymer invited Iris as well. As always he turned up in his Bentley, without which he never went anywhere, and picked me up in Hampstead, with Jean Max. We were to meet Iris somewhere in Chiswick, and take her along to Hampton Court. There she was, waiting, at the agreed spot, and I introduced her to Aymer and Jean-Max. She climbed in. Only then did I notice that she was wearing a diaphanous white silk blouse, something I'd never seen her do before though she'd supposedly been trying to win my love. But to me she would always come in slovenly academic gear, graceless in her wool or sacking dresses, never really seductive, sometimes in the wrong colours (she didn't have the ghost of an aesthetic sense where her own clothes were concerned). I had known her for a couple of years at this stage, and never once had she made an effort to make herself attractive to me by wearing any diaphanous silk blouse. I was so astonished that it took me a while to understand. When we got out in Hampton Court, and sat down in the restaurant at a small table for four, I couldn't hide the truth from myself any more: she had got herself dolled up for Aymer, you could clearly see her breasts, she had a deep décolletage, she seemed almost humble, as though offering herself to the gentleman, but he wasn't the least bit interested, and just thought she was absurd. Over dinner, she talked in her academic way, books were discussed, philosophy touched upon; in his arrogant-superficial way, Aymer had dipped into her little volume on Sartre. Even though she was far too academically articulate, she was rather reticent, intent on not giving Aymer any advantage, not guessing how little he cared what she made of him. He didn't look at her nakedness under the silk blouse—if indeed he even noticed it at all—she had no idea how contemptible she seemed to him, and how uninteresting; moreover, in the arrogant way of the English upper classes, he despised her for being Irish, which she mostly was, but not from the attractive Irish part of Ireland, her father came from Belfast, if I remember correctly, and nothing could have been further from him than a real Paddy, her mother admittedly was somewhat Irish. Jean-Max, who was the most tactful, delicate and sensitive of men, responded to her conversation, there was a lot of talk about Existentialism, at the time no conversation about books was considered complete without that. Jean-Max was courtly to every woman, but in this society Aymer was the lord, and I was the "brains", and there wasn't the least space for Iris. On the way back—we had reached Chiswick again—Aymer failed to ask Iris where she lived. It wasn't a long way for her, she knew Chiswick, she made herself as small as she possibly could, and on the High Street she said "Just drop me here". Aymer braked, she tumbled out of the Bentley onto the pavement in her sheer white silk blouse, and disappeared as fast as she could.

Aymer did not say one word about her, drove off, took me back to Hampstead, her submissiveness filled him with a contempt for her that he never lost, even when she achieved fame in future years—and literary fame was something he wasn't indifferent to. Jean-Max, who was very young, offered a few gracious sentences, which meant little. He didn't say them in French, his English was rather more wooden than the language tends to be anyway. I was deeply unhappy over her appearance and behaviour. She had behaved to Aymer as a person of low class, not only conscious of the class barrier, but acknowledging it, and accepting its application to herself, even as a private citizen, so to speak. Like some silly shop girl, she was out to catch Aymer's eye. She paraded her desire to submit, didn't have the faintest idea how nothing she was to him; any one of his guests, to whom he was always mannerly, meant more to him; I think he did not even see her, in spite of her shimmering blouse; and her form with the huge flat feet and the big legs excluded her from the society of tall, slender, beautiful Englishwomen from the start. But in her comportment, loath though I was to admit it to myself, I recognised a banal, unintellectual, everyday element of feminine calculation. It seemed not even to have crossed her mind to wonder what it might do to me, whom she supposed she knew well.

VAUGHAN WILLIAMS

It is not easy for me to go on writing about these English things. I often find myself shaking with rage when I think of them. My revulsion against a few, a very few, whom I put up with for years and years in London keeps pushing me away each time I think about London. I need to dim part of my recollection, to show the other, which *is* there, in plenty. There were many people there to whom I am grateful that they were as they were. There were others, who sucked my blood, because they weren't slow to notice that I'm prepared to listen to anyone who bemoans his confusion, and on and on.

What I never learned to do, not even in England, was to manage my time. There are people for whom such management amounts to a *raison d'être*. It becomes as important, or more important than their dependants, their spouses, even their pets. More than anyone, I was astounded by Iris, who always had a schedule, even for love, which for her was not a small matter. Perhaps it surprised me even more with her than it did with others, because she liked to insist with great warmth (though there was something about it that rang false), how much she loved one. "You are beautiful!" she would say (when in the grip of desire), and she would say it to people who were anything but beautiful (to myself, for example). I asked myself whether she would have said it to Franz Steiner or to the man who—for many years now—has been her husband. Really, it means nothing (nothing more than: "I'm hungry! Come on!") but since she always avoids unpleasantness, she is bound to call each one of her victims "beautiful".

But there were people who managed their time still better than Iris. A respected left-wing scholar, who wrote a lot for the *New Statesman*, and was once in a Labour government—his name is Douglas Jay—was in the habit of calling in a woman to him, laying his watch on the table, and saying: "I've got five minutes!" (Then he would take off his trousers, expect the woman to do likewise in the same time, and take care of business in three, or *at the most* five minutes. Then she was off. If she was happy with these arrangements, and got by in the allotted time, she might be asked back in a month, not before.) He was married with a wife as long and spindly as himself (as he used to be) and two extremely beautiful daughters.

I often found girls and young women from the well-educated English upper classes breathtakingly beautiful. There were some truly angelic apparitions, as you might imagine them to yourself in winged moments. But mostly they were ice cold, love for them was something mechanical, a custom. At that time, it was no longer *against* the prevailing morality, if anything the opposite. Perhaps that was how they discovered it. Because the ones who were that way inclined, were vehemently so. One woman, whom I knew well, though I didn't love her, had fixed herself up in the following way (following a cold and unhappy marriage to an officer, who died during the War): she lived under one roof with two old men, one of whom, a senior civil servant, was a veritable satyr, and the other, much older, the most wonderful pure man, Ralph Vaughan Williams, the composer and pride of the nation, great-hearted, independent, with no notion of aristocracy, submissive, but without acute rebellion, a man one would like to cover pages and pages about.

It has often puzzled me that great musicians are not better people than they are. In my young days I used to think that the activity by and of itself would make them better people, but this one man, whom I knew for ten or twelve years, remained alive and bright to a great age, and was incapable of a mean thought, let alone a mean action. Such a remark from someone like myself, who takes a sharp view of his fellow men, may seem implausible. But I insist on it: whatever notions one might have of a great-souled man had become truth in this one musician, and that in spite of a fame that lasted for four decades or more.

There is or was an innocence in English life, which no-one can believe who hasn't experienced it for himself. It stands in direct contradiction to a knowledge of music, or a claim thereto. It makes you ask yourself in bewilderment: Is this possible, is this real, is it not the usual pretence? You turn the thing round and round in your head, you listen, you ask (with the best intentions, you *want* to believe it, but still you question). If, after some time, you reach the unshakeable conviction that the man really is as he appears to be, he stays alive for another dozen years, and then is buried in Westminster Abbey.

I have always been profoundly grateful for my two childhood years in England. My father died there, but it wasn't fear that killed him, but his father, and perhaps my mother's obsession with the English language. What he took from England made him happy. What he passed on from the year, barely more, that he was allowed to live in England, became the moral foundation of my life. In 1913, at the age of eight, I left England, drawn away by my mother's restlessness. I didn't return there for another twenty-five years. In the meantime, there was war after war—my jealous love of my mother, the fight for her, for which she never forgave me, the passion for Veza, the friendship with Sonne, the three hard, but comic works from my early manhood, exile from Vienna—but the foundation that I received from my father in England remained intact, it was *moral*, and even today I am not ashamed of calling it that. I spent the rest of my life looking for people who corresponded to such an image, in England I several times came close to finding one, and being reborn as a result. Once, it did happen, and so completely, that I would slap anyone who mouths the platitudes about "Victorian" prudishness.

Sometimes I say the word aloud. I say "England", and I feel as if I've told a lie. My belief in England was absolute at the time I lived there with my father, in my seventh year. He brought me books, I was to read them and talk to him about them, they were the first books I had in my hands, the first books I ever read. He had something to say about each one of the books he brought me, and he expected me to have something to say to him. In the space of a few months, I learned to read in the new language, and if there was anything that brought me happiness, then it was these books my father brought me. Some of them I saw again when I was seventy: there were *Tales from Shakespeare*. A book about William Tell prepared me for Switzerland, a book about Napoleon disposed me against him. *Grimm's Fairy Tales* and the *Arabian Nights* soon followed. I have never lost my hunger for stories and myths. Of *Gulliver's Travels*, I read only the first two parts, about the Lilliputians and the Brobdingnagians. *Robinson Crusoe* taught me solitude and foreign people, Dante taught me justice. (I am still not sure today whether *Don Quixote* was among these books or not. *The Odyssey*, I know, wasn't.)

AYMER

When sadness comes over me, usually in the evenings, I summon up a memory. Even the fact that it *is* a memory helps a little.

Plenty in England was boring, but since it's a memory, it's no longer boring. It glitters when it's produced. It doesn't want it to be night.

But there are things, and people, that fail to glitter, even in memory. Shall I name their names? Better not, they will get in the way of others that want to come to the surface.

Strange, how much time I spend thinking about Aymer, and about Gavin. Perhaps because worlds divided us in biographical and sexual matters.

Perhaps also, because as a pair of jealous brothers—they weren't actually twins—they have something mythic about them. In their childhood, they were given animals that belonged to both of them equally, either because their mother, who gave them these creatures, had wanted to be Christian, or else because they still enjoyed sharing things. Later on, that turned into an incessant battle, and became the focus of their lives, certainly Aymer's. But Gavin contributed as well, because as the younger, he felt disadvantaged, as title, property and most of the money had been settled on the elder brother. After their carefree childhood together, *one* son suddenly found himself the worse off. At first, he immersed himself in paedophilia, and had a lot of success. Aymer tried to match him, and found it much harder. He had to fight for boys who flung themselves at his younger brother, who would proudly show them off, as soon as he had made them his. Aymer wanted to take them away from him—how was he going to take them away from Gavin? With his big Bentley, he terrorised all the local drivers round his estate. He was so dashing, he felt like a racing driver. He took me out with him on a test drive, and I went along, really only to see what the other drivers were like, compared to him. He could buy any car he wanted, no matter how much it cost, and that restored to him his sense of privilege, *vis-à-vis* his brother. He had a racing car, but he didn't have a Bentley, and he couldn't afford to trade it in for anything better once it seemed a bit road-weary. It was pitiful to be with him and watch Aymer roll up in his Bentley. He wouldn't permit himself to arrive any other way. When he hooted outside my flat—I lived on the second floor—I recognised the sound of his horn, and went over to the window. I was never once mistaken, that's how distinctive and incomparable his hooting was.

He often asked me to go travelling with him, and sometimes I accepted. It might mean some fine adventure somewhere in the south. But the driving was unpleasant. We had a target to get to twice daily, and the drive consisted of getting there as quickly as possible. In between, there was nothing, except at mealtimes. We drove at breakneck speed for a few hundred miles, we drove past the most beautiful cities and churches without stopping, because they weren't our destination. The destination had been announced, and that was that. I always sat at his side, and he thought he impressed me with his boldness, he was most astonished when I once said, in the course of a longer conversation, that I hadn't noticed any danger. I was the last person to crave physical bravado—such things didn't exist so far as I was concerned. He admitted in the same conversation how surprised he was by me. If he had been in my place, and I had been driving, he would have forced me to stop, and would have got out of the car. It was only oneself that one could allow to be so reckless while driving. Merely to watch someone else being reckless, and be put at risk by him was intolerable, and he would have put a stop to it, even if it had meant the end of an important friendship. What I remember of our tour is my loss of peace, and the regret over passing so many place names. It was noticed, because it was on the map. But that a town might consist of something more, had done perhaps for hundreds of years, that Burgundy, for example, contains many glories from Roman times, is something one might dream about, but not more. Instead, on the dot of one, it was: "Let's have some food!" And then we drew up outside the premier restaurant of the region, and over lunch I calmly listed everything I hadn't been able to see. He liked to hear that, because even though he respected me, he didn't allow me these things I would have liked to see—and yet I wasn't his arch-rival, his brother, but a friendly ear, and a source of first aid in emotional crises. I don't think he would have respected his own father as much, had he lived. What won his respect was whatever precipitated him into a condition of wordless astonishment. He was inclined—and this was the way with his fellow aristocrats too—to adopt a pose of being bored, although he rarely was. That one might have interest and warmth for anything at all was something he could not grasp, and he assumed it was a particular quality in me that was responsible.

In reality, Aymer was just as sensitive and responsive as I was. How else could I have tolerated him, with all his bad qualities? Happily tolerated him, I should add. He often annoyed me, particularly with his biting scorn of people I respected. But he knew how unimpressed I was by his ancestry. Accustomed to the crazy snobbery of his fellow Englishmen, he had little occasion to speak about it. But he could sense what I thought, as I judged something harshly but silently. He brought it up against himself, as an inner rebuke, whatever he supposed me to be thinking, and even though he consisted of hundreds of flaws and inadequacies, when he was talking to me, he had the sense of being free of them all.

It's impossible for anyone to show more gratitude for what little I gave him, and that yet, for many years, was crucial to him. I can't speak of *time*, because what, with the time-sickness with which, like so many Englishmen, he was afflicted, he felt to be extraordinary generosity on my part, really wasn't: at that time in England, I was happy to give my time to absolutely anyone. For thirty years or more, I was lavish, if not wasteful with it, because I never, not even there, became enslaved to the clock, my time doesn't melt away, any time, spent with anyone speaking about themselves enlarged my sympathies and made me happy, because it meant I wasn't forced to keep my own company, and to me that is happiness, to be with others and not alone, to be able to depart from one's self, without being on one's best behaviour, yes, without even really being aware of the fact.

I must add that in the course of the three trips I went on with Aymer, I was able to leave myself in the most complete and natural way, in Morocco, in Provence and in Greece. It must be due to him that these trips meant more to me than any others. What nowadays must seem to be little or nothing to most people, to me was more than everything. That must be to do with the fact that he always wanted to do something with me, to be able to observe me. Whether it was him who was speaking, or me who was listening to others.

ENGLAND, AN ISLAND

During the War, more than fifty years ago now, it was England's salvation that it was an island. It was still an island, and that asset, a colossal advantage, has been frittered away.

Today, it is what's left over from a government whose one and only prescription for everything was selfishness. People felt proud of the fact, as though it were some kind of revelation, a horde of men (and women) in pinstripes swarmed over the land, calling themselves businessmen or executives, and sought to plunder the country, just as once the country had sought to plunder the rest of the world. England decided it would loot itself, and engaged an army of yuppies for that end. As a paradise, but one to be had here and now, everyone was promised their own house. People got busy, and, with quite un-English haste, made their piles. The state proudly declared it would no longer provide for anything, because everyone was to provide for themselves, and who goes around cleaning other people's streets? The hypocrisy, which was actually the mortar that held English society together, fell away. In seemingly no time at all, the universal slogan was look after number one, and devil take the hindmost. It was shown—I say this with incredulity—that selfishness was every bit as much worth preaching as selflessness. The supreme preacher in the country was a woman who tirelessly rejected whatever was done for other people. For other people, everything was too expensive; for oneself, nothing was. Water, air, light, were turned into businesses, to flourish or fail; usually they failed. A small war was started on the other side of the globe, to remind the waves that they were Britannia's. The person of Churchill was invoked, and the great danger in which England had found itself not so many years ago; and what made it all still more effective was the fact that these tough decisions were taken by a woman who was married to a simple (in every sense) millionaire. He had settled for too little, she hadn't. He kept to the shadows, and didn't get in the way. Because of her, the cities collapsed into disgusting squalor. The schools rotted, so that children might learn to trust instead to their own acumen and hard-heartedness. Things that other politicians had put forward, half in jest—because the other half still had something to say—were rapidly put into practice. Since every man is inclined to meanness, and only restrains himself with some difficulty, English humanity now felt a huge sense of relief, because all at once they were permitted to be as mean as any other people, and receive the highest praise for it on top of that.

I was permitted to live through this time, and see my best friends warped. They came from nurseries that any citizen of any country in the world would have licked his lips to have been at. To them, a governess, who played the opposite of the games they had been raised to play, was a boon. Suddenly, you were *supposed* to be all the disgusting things that a man naturally is, but has had to renounce. The relief must have been incredible, and all that was left of the old hypocrisy was a show of pretence towards me. There were of course others, and not the worst, who showed themselves to me the way they really were. They knew what I thought, and respected it. I have nothing to accuse them of, beyond their noxious human nature, of which I myself stand accused just as much. But I am angry with the others who were dearer to me, sensitive, delicate beings among them, poets and authors, or at least writers, who, for a time of ten years or more, worshipped that idol from the days of slavery, and in my presence continued to use all the language of philanthropy.

There was worse: there were the surprises. There were close friends I hadn't seen for some years, who suddenly met me in the full glare of their new convictions. They felt innocent, because, from the moment of their conversion, some little time had passed. They had made careers for themselves, they had become rich and famous, and of course they were going to stick up for themselves. They disguised themselves so little that they were shocked by my dismay. Among them were emotional women, who were dripping with money in their own private lives, but in public endorsed the preacher of selfishness, even as it was already becoming clear that she was heading for catastrophe. Then there was grief for the country, which you didn't love any the less because you owned a piece of it, which you didn't want to risk losing, in theory.

There were also historical routes into the new situation of the country. A woman historian to whom I owe a great deal in my life, a woman of positively French intellectual adroitness, from one of the leading intellectual and scientific families in the country, an expert on the seventeenth century, full of pride in the literature of the Elizabethan period immediately preceding, surprised me—I hadn't seen her for five or six years—with an enthusiastic speech on England's new Elizabethan period, now, under the governess. She was completely convinced, she was exuberant and myopic, I was speechless—and for the first time in the forty-five years of our friendship, I kept a gloomy silence, and let her know what I thought of her dementia.

SPEED

What else is there to say about Aymer and his cult of speed? Impatience was his governing characteristic. He had acquired it over decades, waiting for the death of his grandfather, from whom he was to inherit the title and the estate. Perhaps he thought his fast driving would get him there sooner. There was always something murderous about it. The Bentley was so powerful that in a collision it would crush anyone else. The driver, meanwhile, was safe. So he drove around the country in his murderous way, and nothing happened. When the time finally came, he had got used to it, and he continued to drive. He was bored in his castle at home; out in the world, as long as he was at the wheel, there were always adventures. Nothing impressed the young men whose eye he was trying to catch so much as his Bentley. It did for him what armour did for the knights of old.

But Aymer's real secret was his *stammer*. I don't know how old he was when it began, I never asked him. He had an inferiority complex, and would start to stammer when in full flow. Thereby he would also interrupt the person he was talking to, his notional superior. He forced him to adjust to his own speed. It was his way of regulating the speed of the conversation. In many cases, he was successful, and he viewed those people as vassals. For those that weren't cowed by it, who failed to observe his stammer, he had reverence. It was a reverence at whose bars he was continually shaking, but only to be able to hold on to them.

I saw a painting of Vaughan Williams, almost by chance, a very late portrait by some Royal Academician, completely *null* as a painting, assembled from photographs, and hence such a likeness that he leapt off the page at me. He has to be in this book about England. I have nothing to say about his music, I only know some of it, perhaps it is insignificant, I don't know, anyway, it doesn't matter.

It won't be easy, because I can't possibly tell the wonderful and hilarious story of his Ursula, through whom I first met him, and her Falstaff, who was, so to speak, part of the furniture of this marriage, who lived in the house of this wonderful man. I can only talk about these things, never publish them. But how charming it would be to think the noble old man *knew* it all, and had the greatness of heart to approve it, or at least tolerate it, for her sake, because he didn't want to be without her in his old years.

Two things are always in my mind when I think about my book on England: Aubrey's *Brief Lives*, how I would love to write something comparable, because I *could*, I know I could, and second, English arrogance. It seems that that was the most striking thing about England all along, the actual *product* of English life, which I saw at full stretch when it saved the world from Hitler, and then in the following decades, in its apparently unstoppable decay.

SOME VARIETIES OF ARROGANCE

The nakedest and unhappiest, because least effective instance of it: that of *Aymer*, whom I knew better than I knew anyone in my life. With him, arrogance is connected to property and rank; but also with the knowledge that in spite of his lofty (ducal) origins, he is strictly speaking on the lowest rung of the hierarchy, a mere baronet. The connection in his mother, Lady Mary, the Duke's daughter, between this arrogance and truly Christian humility as a member of Edward Irving's Catholic Apostolic Church.

Strangest of all, her daughter *Christine*, Aymer's sister, a member, an active member, of the Communist Party, which in England has remained so small as to retain something of the character of a sect. A party at Christine's, everyone either aristocrats or Communists, the strangest party I ever went to. I knew almost no-one there, a bare handful, by name, and when I talked to people for the first time, I couldn't tell if they were aristocrats or Communists. From their intellectual tone, they could have been either, even though here, at Christine's party, the Communists had let fall their usual masks. Of course, the two were truly allied during the War.

The arrogance of *T. S. Eliot*, the acquisition, so to speak, of an American returned to the home country after many generations. It will be difficult to describe Eliot as the quite abysmal character he was. It is not enough to point to his insolent description of Goethe, and his inhuman and unpoetlike verdict on Blake. His costive-minimal work (so many spittoons of failure), the poet in England and among the Modernists of emotional impoverishment, which through him became fashionable. The hierarchy he (in imitation of Dante) imported into literary criticism, to find himself a place at the top table. So successful was he that he got away with his feeble plays, which were taken seriously, and not just in Germany.

Oxford arrogance, something Chinese about it, but that is really the only attractive thing about it. Inexhaustible in its sterility. But the most astonishing library (the Bodleian) and the most astonishing bookshop (Blackwell's) in the world. The rigid philosophy of the schoolmen, which came out of Oxford. Cambridge I hardly knew, but it occurs to me that a very lively, serious, eloquent, moral, and still witty figure came from there: Bertrand Russell.

(What would England be without the Irish immigration!) Continual influx of Irish, as into the US, but for them, the victorious English would be destitute (who already were able to draw on the Welsh).Was any one of the people I knew in England truly free of arrogance?

Herbert Read (who later, on his wife's account, accepted a knighthood).

Vaughan Williams, the composer, whom I knew as an old man, perfectly intact, inexhaustible and indestructible.

One might say—up to a point—that *Bertrand Russell* wasn't actually steeped in arrogance. All his life he sought to oppose his background. Also, he was too much the randy buck to be arrogant.

Dylan Thomas, but he was a Welshman and a poet, a poet of

plenty, not of impoverishment, like Eliot. He never struck me as arrogant, though Caitlin, his wife, did.

Veronica saved her arrogance for her historiography. Her parties were such fiascos that you can't really describe her as arrogant. Her ambition was grotesque, but it stemmed from the fact that her mother had not wanted her, and from the fact that men found her unattractive. She knew all the little byways of fame, and wasn't above using them for herself, but I don't think she ever crushed anyone by her arrogance.

Iris. Not really arrogant in the English way either, she is after all Irish. She took on board Oxford and Cambridge, along with the schoolman philosophy of those places, and of course she is as ambitious as a master-criminal. But she's too fixated on love to be arrogant, she wants practically everyone she meets—man, woman, whatever—to be in love with her.

In the case of *Ursula*, her undoubted arrogance was sugared over with kind-heartedness, and so never made itself manifest. Her desire—right up to her high old age—to please played a part as well.

Clement looked like a Roman Apollo, and knew it, and that made her appear arrogant, though she was no more so than many others.

Margaret, very arrogant (though Viennese on her mother's side), also mean, she always had money, and in that very English way kept saying: "I can't afford it." Whenever anyone in England came out with that sentence *early* in a conversation—prophylactically, so to speak—then you knew they were rich.

English things seem to spread themselves before me, more with every passing day. Perhaps I'm no longer so overpowered by the grief I've felt since February 1984. I am once more capable of coherent thoughts about Hampstead. Perhaps also my shock

Clement Glock

at Carol's letter, which hit me a year and a half ago, and still continues to resonate.

In my memory, England has faded; at the same time, everything that happened there in more than forty years is suddenly present, as though it had merely been waiting to appear in its fullness. I still can't see any organisation in this memoir, but it is full of people, language, destinies, offence and emotion. A few seem to have become still nobler than they were, others have been dunked in pitch and are making vain efforts to reach the surface. I will talk about that too to anyone who will listen, I will talk about it much too much, until—to my consternation—people turn away in boredom. That country really isn't the centre of the world any more, though people are still amazed—I more amazed than ever—by its literature.

The *chance nature* of your meetings in England. That would

be good. But in the course of so many years, something else has come of that: a *hierarchy*, governed by your antipathies and hurts, what an unjust and skewed portrait that will make, of a country that is now stuck in its deepest wretchedness: its best institutions, which once were models to the rest of the world, now in pieces: cast into question and shattered by the ten years in which the claque of the apostles of selfishness were in power.

It is something I cannot quite believe: the country going to the dogs, not through any foreign occupation and oppression, but by its own volition and choice.

Should I relate its *idyllic* condition, of fifty years ago? Who would believe me? Who would care? That would take the serenity of old age, which I don't possess, or only sometimes, all too rarely.

Elias Canetti in Hampstead Cemetery

AFTERWORD

I really came to England to learn how to write German . . .

LICHTENBERG

C anetti's English memoirs caused a sensation when they first came out in Germany. His anger at what he considered the faults of English life might have been enough to ensure attention, but his broadside against the literary scene seemed designed to shock. Few German-speaking writers have equalled his knowledge of modern England. None had a sharper tongue when it came to expressing his views.

Canetti first began to tell the story of his life in a trilogy covering the years 1905–35. Compared to the violent energy of the books that had first made his reputation, the novel *Auto da Fé* and the anthropological study *Crowds and Power*, the autobiographies seemed surprisingly Augustan. Their vivid, precise style lent the vanished past an almost sensuous immediacy. Moving effortlessly between anecdotes and analysis, reflection and observation, Canetti provided an easy entrée to a difficult life. It was this new, approachable classicism, schooled in the writings of Goethe and Stendhal, that contributed to the autobiography's popular success. When it came to depicting his personal development amid the turmoil and violence of early twentieth-century Central Europe, notwithstanding his own former iconoclasm, Canetti performed his task as if he were writing a German

Bildungsroman. He seemed to gloss over many problems and tensions of his "real life". In their place he set up what is perhaps the most remarkable literary portrait gallery in twentieth-century writing: Kraus, Musil, Brecht, Broch and many others parade through his pages like trophies as Canetti seeks to assure himself of his own place among the stars. By repeated mirrorings, the "figures" he describes—to use one of his favourite concepts—reflect aspects of his own nature. When he portrays another character, whether a celebrity or an obscure acquaintance, we glimpse a new aspect of his own personality. This reflectivity is an important device for endowing his memories with clear contours and a fixed form. When he enters into other people, the writer who had for many years understood himself as a "master of transformations" enacts his own, final metamorphosis.

As a classic autobiographer, Canetti sets himself in relation to the great events of the day. Like Goethe, who depicts himself in heroic terms at the siege of Mainz in his *Campaign in France* and elsewhere glorifies his own insights into the "historic" character of the Battle of Valmy, or like Stendhal who lets Fabrice in *La Chartreuse de Parme* experience Napoleon's fall at Waterloo, in the second volume of his autobiography Canetti evokes the burning of Vienna's Palace of Justice—a key moment on the Austrian road to dictatorship—to lay claim to his own place in history, and to show the importance of history on his development. However, the omission of certain other events and opinions (like his leftist politics, which can only be deduced from such details as his presence in Brecht's Berlin circle) created the impression that Canetti wanted to transfigure the picture of his earlier life. Facts such as his plan to contribute to the anti-Nazi journal *Das Wort*, which was published in Moscow around 1936, are omitted, as is the assistance he and his wife gave to Ernst Fischer after the latter was beaten up in street fighting by the Nazis. Fischer and others on the left were upset by what they regarded as a betrayal, and attacked Canetti publicly for his stance. Other readers, however, detected a gentleness in the memoirs that typified Canetti the friend as distinct from Canetti the writer—this more attractive side to his personality, incidentally, is captured in Veza Canetti's novel *The Tortoises.*

His critics overlooked that a writer's autobiography is a lived fiction, a literary act not to be measured by the same standards as a scholarly biography. Canetti is interested in a symbolic representation of his life, not in historical exactitude, let alone in life as it is lived. Hence his tacit response to his critics in an aphorism he wrote in 1993:

> *The story of a life should contain many puzzles and leave much to guesswork . . . Some things should be presented in such a way that their nature is always concealed . . . The story of a life is as secret as life itself. A life that can be explained is no life at all.*

When he formulated this aphorism, it now turns out, Canetti was already at work on a continuation of his life story. As he told some of his friends, the autobiography was originally planned as a work in five volumes. Each part was centred on a particular sense, as the three titles suggest: *The Tongue Set Free, The Torch in My Ear, The Play of the Eyes.* The emblems indicate the development of the whole man—the traditional theme of a *Bildungsroman.*

The new volume, now published as *Party in the Blitz*, was just possibly conceived in terms of the sense of smell—in which case the nose would have been its emblem—given Canetti's reference to the "smell of weakness" he encountered in England; but it seems more likely that he was thinking in terms of touch or feeling, in which case a pun on the hand or heart might have been expected in the title. This would have linked up with Canetti's repeated references to the coldness and the lack of feeling he encountered among the English. Be that as it may, the symbolic references to the senses in *Party in the Blitz* imply a connection between this late work and the earlier autobiographies. But the book is also very much a new departure, both in subject and in theme, not to mention the vigour, the unrestrained acerbity with which Canetti lays out his views. The Olympian calm and the self-censorship of the previous autobiography is set aside for a manner altogether more spirited.

Canetti was eighty-five when he began work on these memoirs, having finally left London for Zurich about a decade before.

The first note for the new project simply reads: "Memories from England.—London, Thursday, 11 October 1990.—As long as my eyes permit, I still want to write something about my time in England." Eleven days later he lights on the angle: "22 October 1990.—At last I have found what I would like to write about England, my English period: Amersham and the time during the War." This is the time of his evacuation. But there is a problem. "So many names have disappeared. Will I still be able to find the people? I can see them before me, even without their names. I would like to think first of the ones who were not too close to me, otherwise the book will simply become my private story again. What I'd now like to do is to give a picture of country life in England as it was during the War." By the beginning of the following year, he had succumbed to uncertainty: "2 January 1991.—There are so many of them in my memory, who shall I begin with?" Despite his doubts, though, Canetti completed a first draft in October 1991. That manuscript is now known as A.

This first draft served as a basis for a second version, which Canetti announced as follows: "Friday 17 July 1992—It is time for me to turn to England again because I feel how things are slowly disappearing, even the early ones, and it would be dreadful if suddenly nothing remained of forty years in England." Another note reads: "I began to write down my memories of England under the title 'London'. I continued that version in October 1990 and then again in January 1991. Then I interrupted my work and began again in earnest on 17 July 1992." Less than a month later he finished, describing his manuscript thus: "Out of England—provisional, unedited draft (not to be published in this form)—17 July to 23 August 1992." This, then, is the second manuscript, now known as B. It is by far the largest draft and constitutes the major part of the book published as *Party in the Blitz*.

There were two more major periods of work. From February to April and then again from August to November in 1993 Canetti produced a large number of further notes as well as diary entries that contain many passages devoted to England. This is version C. Apart from various fragments and sketches the material includes longer sections in which Canetti tries to give an overview of his experiences.

Finally, he took up work again in 1994, dictating about half of the second manuscript (B) to his daughter, Johanna, who produced the first typescript. This is version D. However, none of the manuscripts was finished, and the project remained incomplete when Canetti died later that year, in August 1994, at the age of 89.

By the time of its abandonment the work had grown far

beyond the original intention to concentrate on Canetti's time in Amersham. This becomes clear from the structure he eventually envisaged: "I have to distinguish between the first years and the early phase of the War, the later time in Amersham and then the later and longest time in Hampstead. I really need to keep these different periods apart." He never managed to. When he stopped work, Amersham had given way to London as the centre of attention, and—in the best tradition of English travel writing—the focus had expanded to include an obligatory visit to Scotland. The autobiographical sketch had become a panorama of English life. But Canetti was not entirely happy about what he had produced. Something about England seemed to elude him: "When I write about England, I notice how wrong it all is."

Perhaps this had something to do with the different perspectives that he was trying to master. During the early years in England, he had come to see himself as an Englishman. He became a British citizen, and felt the part. As he wrote to Marie-Louise von Motesiczky around 1951: "I can't help it, but I now feel completely at home in England, especially in London. I can now become an Englishman with a good conscience. I feel how I react to the French here as an Englishman, and not as before as a Viennese, a Swiss, or a man from the Balkans." By the time he came to write the memoirs, however, he had gone through so many changes in his literary life—the obscurity of an émigré; the celebrity of *Auto da Fé*; the equivocal reception of *Crowds and Power*; the success in Germany and Austria; the renewed neglect in England; the Nobel Prize—that it is hardly surprising he could not always disentangle the different phases. Turning this to advantage, he imbued some of his most striking recollections with knowledge gained from multiple perspectives. Sometimes affection dominates. At others, spleen. On occasion, as has been noted, he resembles a figure in one of his own aphorisms: "In taking leave, he determined to insult everybody who was close to him. He insulted those people the most whom he had loved the longest."

When reading Canetti's notes, one is struck by the way he talks of his late friends and acquaintances as if they were living beings who must be preserved from oblivion. Autobiography was a means to conquer death, a part of his plan to outwit mortality. He hated death, and believed that humanity's greatest task lay in overcoming it. Both his writing in general and his literary estate in particular formed part of this battle for survival. In earlier years, he claimed to have left many works unfinished so that he would not have to publish them, anticipating that they would be found and edited posthumously. Print would ensure survival. Hence, even if *Party in the Blitz* originally appeared without his explicit consent, he would have expected its appearance.

There has been some discussion about whether *Party in the Blitz* should have been published at all, so perhaps the issue should be dealt with here. Canetti was clear about what should be done with his estate, and the German edition of the book followed his guidelines. His will stipulates that no new writings of his should be published until eight years after his death, i.e. not before 2002, and that personal material (letters and diaries) should remain unpublished for a further twenty-two years, i.e. until 2024. Accordingly, the published edition of *Party in the Blitz* omits all the diary entries contained in the manuscripts, presenting only the sections that clearly belong to the autobiography. Canetti would no doubt have wanted to give the work a more polished form, but whilst some parts are obviously intended as an aide-memoire, and are here included for the light they shed on his intentions, others are already well-turned pieces, complete in themselves. More details about the composition of the volume will be found in the note on the text (on page 236).

Having presented himself as a Central European intellectual in the three volumes of his autobiography, a contemporary of Kraus, Musil, Broch and Brecht, in *Party in the Blitz* Canetti describes his life as an émigré. In many respects his story differed greatly from that of the other writers who found refuge in England in the 1930s. I cannot think of another German-speaking author of his generation, and certainly none who remained faithful to German as his literary language, who made himself quite so much at home on the English literary scene as Canetti did. Others, such as Franz Baermann Steiner, might have known more about English literature; yet others, notably Michael Hamburger, established themselves as English writers. Canetti, however, remained a German writer but became accepted as a figure on the London scene. The many writers he does mention are only a small proportion of his friends and acquaintances. We know that he was familiar with a host of others, among them Dannie Abse and Ted Hughes, and that Salman Rushdie was among the novelists who turned up on his doorstep. Exiles from other dictatorships, too, such as the Portuguese novelist Helder Macedo who lived round the corner from him in Hampstead, also have their stories to relate about Canetti.

He knew everyone. And everyone knew him. This is all the more remarkable since initially he did not owe his reputation to his publications, but rather to the force of his personality. As he laments in this memoir, when he arrived there was not a soul in England—with the single exception of Arthur Waley—who knew his writing. No doubt the complaint smacks of vanity.

But Canetti uses his personal perspective to make a point about English society. The hierarchies he detected in England demanded public achievements as markers of rank. Without the aura bestowed by birth, by publication or by profession, according to Canetti intellectuals in England have little chance of social success. Every meeting in England involves the implicit question "how high" or "how low" on the social scale is one's interlocutor ranked? Iris Murdoch remarked Canetti's problem ironically in *The Flight from the Enchanter* where she turns him into a character who is famous without anybody knowing exactly what he is famous *for*. However, as Canetti now reveals in his memoirs, during the English years he was consciously looking for people to write about, acting as what he calls a "secret historian" or a "spy". He made a conscious effort to meet people. In France, he went in pursuit of Picasso. In cafés across Europe, he initiated conversations with complete strangers, often using his own work as a pretext. As he used to say half-jokingly, he wanted to be the "dog of my day"—*der Hund meiner Zeit*.

Even though the manuscripts remain incomplete, it seems clear that Canetti planned to underpin his personal observations with a systematic structure. He aims to produce his panorama of English life by depicting a carefully chosen sample of figures, ranging from a road sweeper to members of the British aristocracy, but concentrating on a representative sample of artists and intellectuals.

I, then, was more a listener than an analyst, and I was given so much to listen to that I could fill hundreds of volumes with it, if I could remember it. Even the portion that I did remember was sufficient for several books, but I wouldn't even think of going to such a source. All I am interested in is

having a few people come to life that at that time became
characters to me [in German, Canetti uses the term
Figuren], *and have remained so, even though I haven't*
thought about them for decades. I want to free myself of this
excess of English personalities [again, he uses that word
Figuren]. *But I will only choose those that seem to me typical.*
I would like them, put together, to make up a portrait of
England as it was in the middle of the century.

The variety of his English acquaintances is impressive.
Politicians like the Conservative Enoch Powell and the Labour
minister Douglas Jay, intellectuals like Bertrand Russell and
Herbert Read, scholars and scientists like Arthur Waley and J.
D. Bernal, women intellectuals like C. V. Wedgwood and
Diana Spearman, writers and poets like Iris Murdoch and
Kathleen Raine, the collector and painter Roland Penrose, the
sculptor Henry Moore, the composer Ralph Vaughan
Williams—Canetti's gallery documents the cultural riches of
the English years, and his ambition to treat specific individuals
as representative types. He is particularly keen to demonstrate
his relationship to England's major poets, T. S. Eliot (whom he
knew only slightly) and Dylan Thomas (whom he knew better
than the memoirs indicate). It is odd that despite his own
efforts as a playwright he does not include any dramatists (one
wonders for example whether he knew Christopher Frye. Did
he meet John Osborne?) and even more surprising that he does
not include a novelist. (Did he know E. M. Forster? Did he
meet Evelyn Waugh or Anthony Powell?) There is a
tantalising reference to Virginia Woolf—his use of her
Christian name indicates that he met her—but that is all we
have to go on. In the absence of other writers, his friend and
sometime lover Iris Murdoch has to do duty as both

philosopher and novelist.

Canetti's emphasis on English life leads him to omit several people from his own émigré circle whom one might have expected to appear in a more faithful autobiographical memoir. Apart from the poet and anthropologist Franz Baermann Steiner and the painter Oskar Kokoschka, he hardly presents any refugees. We know, however, that he was on friendly terms with the poets Michael Hamburger and Erich Fried (until he broke with the latter because of his attacks on the State of Israel), with the biologist and artist Erna Pinner, the art historian E. H. Gombrich, the painter Milein Cosman and her husband, the music critic Hans Keller. Yet he does not attempt to recreate this vanished émigré world, a task that awaits some later writer. He also largely excludes his own private life, his family, and his most intimate friends: his wife Veza hardly figures, her brother Bucky Calderon barely rates a mention. By and large, the women he loved also play minor roles: the sculptor Anna Mahler, the writer Friedl Benedikt and the painter Marie-Louise von Motesiczky. Apart from Amersham, whither he moved at Marie-Louise's suggestion, details about where he lived, or the fact that he also kept rooms in friends' houses, play no part in this book. Likewise, the poverty that Canetti and Veza suffered, the struggle for financial survival, and the difficult path to acceptance in post-war Germany hardly obtrude. Some of Canetti's bitterness can perhaps be explained by the "humiliations" he suffered as an émigré, which he says he was expected to regard as "kindnesses". This whole theme and the question of how he coped with ordinary life is omitted. That helps him place the emphasis very much on England and the English. However, frequent references to the idea of the "crowd" do suggest his preoccupation with *Crowds and Power*, the *magnum opus* to which both Canetti and Veza sacrificed their lives as novelists. The very first chapter of that study, dealing with the fear of contact, can now be directly related to the English experience.

Even though Canetti does not focus particularly on the émigré world, his memoirs correct the received image of literary Hampstead as quintessentially English, a former village on the hilly ground in the north of London that had provided a gathering place for artists and intellectuals for more than two centuries. It became a popular summer resort because of its fresh air and its spa waters, and today still retains much of its village character. Coming here in the eighteenth century, Defoe felt "closer to Heaven"; London's most noted literary club, the Kit-Cat, chose Hampstead for its summer meetings; and painters such as Hogarth and Gainsborough also frequented the area. Key Hampstead moments in the Romantic era include the meeting between Coleridge and Keats near Kenwood House—Coleridge complained about the racket kicked up by the nightingales, Keats dedicated one of his finest poems to them. Wordsworth and Coleridge tramped together across the Heath. So did Dickens and Wilkie Collins. As London expanded in the twentieth century many more writers and artists moved to the leafy north, including D. H. Lawrence, Katherine Mansfield, Agatha Christie and Daphne du Maurier. A shift occurred in the 1930s when Hampstead became home to several thousand German-speaking refugees, drawn to its affordable housing and artistic atmosphere. By the early 1940s a staggering 25,000 "aliens" lived in Hampstead and its surrounds, i.e. about 45 per cent of the local population. What Louis MacNeice called "the guttural sorrow of the refugees" pervaded the district—people as noticeable for their looks and accents as any other immigrant group, and often similarly welcome.

If Canetti was from the start a prince of the intellect, he was not initially a prominent figure, not even among the exiles. Other Hampstead residents, notably Freud, who came from Vienna in 1938 and died in 1939, were better known—no doubt to Canetti's chagrin: he squares up to him in these memoirs, scorning the psychoanalytic school he simply calls "analysts". Yet other figures, such as the dramatist Ernst Toller, one of the most notable German intellectuals to oppose the Nazis, were far better connected on arrival. In his Hampstead years, from 1934 to 1936, Toller drew on the support of Virginia Woolf, Aldous Huxley, H. G. Wells and Bertrand Russell. Yet others played a bigger part in émigré politics, including the Hampstead writer Robert Neumann; or they worked for the BBC in the war of the airwaves, as did Hans Flesch-Brunningen. Canetti observed this world as a participant, and although he does not portray it as such, the select group his memoirs depict includes some key émigré figures. Fred Uhlman, Oskar Kokoschka and even Franz Steiner all played a part in the exile scene, its social life, its clubs, its political associations. Uhlman founded the Free German League of Culture at his house in Hampstead, with Kokoschka as its president. When the League became exclusively Marxist in outlook, José Rehfisch, Grete Fischer and others seceded to start the non-political *Club 43* close by in Belsize Park. Canetti knew both organisations. When presenting his view of the British, therefore, despite his idiosyncracies, Canetti's perspective does reflect this wider, highly stratified community, as well as its complex attitudes: affection, gratitude and admiration for the island race, tempered on occasion by the frustrations, incomprehension and even resentment felt by the alien. With time, the exiles merged into the host community, and yet throughout the period Canetti writes about, there were some strong, even surprising continuities: whilst researching *Crowds and Power*, Canetti was surely as conscious of the ghost of his personal rival, Freud, who had lived just down the road, as of that of Karl Marx, yet another exile to enjoy British liberty, who had lived not far away in North London when writing *Das Kapital*—in some ways no doubt Canetti's model for a book that was meant to change the world; and when he and Veza observed the Battle of Britain from Hampstead Heath, they probably stood in almost the same spot as D. H. Lawrence and Frieda, who in 1915 had here watched a German Zeppelin attacking London. Lawrence's reaction reads like a premonition of the Blitz: "Guns boomed and searchlights raked the sky and fires burned far off in the city."

Canetti and Veza had close links with England before they settled here in February 1939. They both knew English well, and this eased their acculturation. True, she had a Viennese accent—which she liked to exaggerate for comic effect—and he spoke English as he spoke every language—correctly, but with a distinctive Central European timbre. In Vienna, they had earned a living by translating from the English (e.g. Upton Sinclair's novels, which were published by the left-wing Malik Verlag), and they also had family ties in England. Veza's brother lived in the south of England, whilst Canetti himself had first come over as a child, living in Manchester with his parents. Indeed, the sense that among his multiple personalities Canetti felt himself to be in some way an Englishman was reinforced by the fact narrated in *The Tongue Set Free* that English was the first language which he learned to read. The books he encountered as a child in Manchester helped to shape his literary identity—among them *Robinson Crusoe, Gulliver's Travels* and a translation of the *Arabian*

Nights. It was here too that he had that seminal experience (narrated in the first volume of his autobiography) when his father collapsed and died in the presence of his wife and children. Canetti does not touch on this trauma in *Party in the Blitz*, but it may be that the early emotional wound, which lay behind his life-long struggle against death, may explain some of the animosity he later encountered when coming to terms with English life.

When they arrived in February 1939, the War was imminent, and it is omnipresent in the earlier years of *Party in the Blitz*, if never fully described. Rather, Canetti follows it in the concrete details that touch him immediately—at the party in the Blitz, in the anxieties of his hosts at Amersham, on a bus ride. The ambiguity of his own position as a pacifist never comes up. Although many non-combatants—Wittgenstein, Canetti's friend Franz Baermann Steiner—saw it as their duty to play their part in the war effort, Canetti never seems to have felt obliged to do his bit other than as a writer, and never examines his conscience to question his behaviour. But nor does he boast about his moral stand. The fact, not dwelt on here, that he abjured all creative writing during the War in effect ended his career as a novelist; the fact that he refused to publish until the cessation of hostilities further impeded his progress; and the fact that out of principle he refused to work for money, waiting until his recognition as a writer brought its own rewards, condemned him to a life that was frequently on the breadline. If he and Veza sometimes starved, this resulted from their own moral stance, what Canetti would have regarded as their "secret", and does not form any part of his story here. By the same token, when recollecting the worst horrors of the war years, he does not dwell on his own feelings, but objectifies them in the moving response of the street sweeper. It is left to the reader to trace the effect of these terrible events on his writing.

Canetti's later thinking relates every human and historical phenomenon back to the individual human being. He espouses a fairly sober humanism, which—by-passing the post-war debate on humanism conducted by Sartre and Heidegger—returns to its roots in the Renaissance. The principal model he names for his method is the English antiquary, John Aubrey, a writer who experienced what Canetti regards as the greatest period of English culture. Aubrey often laments the customs destroyed by the Civil War, which, he believes, constituted the greatest historical change since the Romans. Aubrey is perhaps now best remembered for his *Lives*, 426 short biographies. More than a hundred of them were edited a few years after the Second World War by Oliver Lawson Dick, and published as *Aubrey's Brief Lives*. Writing at a similarly momentous juncture in history, when constructing his own autobiography Canetti tried to emulate Aubrey as a biographer. His portrait recalls Aubrey's brevity, his directness, his sense of the grotesque.

According to Lawson Dick, Aubrey was the first writer to eschew moral judgements in his biographies. He could conjure up a personality with a single anecdote or simply by listing a set of facts. His love of minor details, and even of apparent trivia, lends his collection extraordinary vitality. Writing of Francis Bacon, he simply notes: "He was a *pederast*. His Ganimeds and Favourites took bribes; but his Lordship always gave judgement *secundum aequum et bonum* [according to what was just and good]." He is just as blunt about Descartes: "He was too wise a man to encomber himselfe with a Wife; but as he was a man, he had the desires and appetites of a man; he therefore kept a good conditioned hansome woman that he liked, and by whom he had some Children (I think 2 or 3)." Canetti borrows Aubrey's manner of noting a few telling details to vividly create a character. With a similar straightforwardness he describes the Maxwells' competitive pederasty, and the unusual marital relations in the Vaughan Williams and Empson households. What is new about Canetti's method is his attempt to merge Aubrey's individualising manner with Theophrastus' style of creating types in order to construct an autobiography. His figures stand out as unique individuals whom he has known. He also gives them certain general human traits. Besides, his shrewd eye for sexual constellations and marital relations among the British reveals the armchair anthropologist familiar with the writings of Margaret Mead and Bronislaw Malinowski. This educated mix contributes to the work's very individual flavour, part memoir, part satire, part anthropology. As in Canetti's aphorisms, the English memoirs also betray the presence of Georg Christoph Lichtenberg (another German-speaking visitor to England) as a shaping influence on his style.

The careful reader will see through the portraits and recognise Canetti himself in the mirrorings and corre spondences, the repetitions and reversals. Whether one thinks of Bertrand Russell's art of questioning, Herbert Read's invisibility, J. D. Bernal's Communism, the street sweeper's manner of holding a conversation, Mr Milburn's devouring strange intellectual systems, or indeed Hetta Empson's sexual libertarianism, Canetti's portraits mirror his own metamorphoses, and his own complex humanity.

The narrative creates a subtle web of associations through which Canetti locates himself on the English scene. His listing of his favourite authors, for example, suggests how much his work owes to English literature. Take the references to Hobbes. *Leviathan* constitutes a response to the political turmoil of Hobbes' age, and we know that Canetti's *Crowds and Power* was conceived in a similar spirit. Indeed, it seems that Hobbes' philosophy must have influenced Canetti more than he ever allows. In *Crowds and Power*, he seems to have adopted Hobbes' concept of society as "*bellum omnium contra omnes*" as well as his view that society was not based on man's sociability, but on the fear of a violent death, what Hobbes calls "*metus mortis violentiae*". Thus the new volume of Canetti's autobiography, if we can call it that, establishes a link between the political philosopher of the English Revolution, and the émigré thinker who set out to oppose the War. He invested so much of his life and energy into *Crowds and Power* that he experienced later wars, such as the Falklands War and the Gulf War, as a personal failure—the failure of his book to prevent bloodshed. This intellectual hubris, incidentally, is mirrored in his account of Kokoschka's despair at his failure to prevent the Second World War.

Canetti's way of writing in these memoirs often recalls the diary form. That may have something to do with the fact that we are dealing with a fragment. As I have suggested, Canetti would surely have revised some sections. Nonetheless, the whole tendency of his project seems to be to transfer the truthful immediacy we associate with a diary to the more reflective form of autobiography. That can be inferred from an essay he wrote on the diary: the very same qualities he attributes to the diary form reappear in the autobiography. In the essay, he emphasises the "violence" of his nature, "which really consists of exaggeration"; yet, as he says, in his diary he does not "combat" this propensity, because "he is concerned with emphasis, with the sharpness and concreteness of everything that makes up a life". Moments of "agitation" and things one is "ashamed" about must be written down. People should preserve their faults, and not idealise themselves. This attitude to the mind, which Canetti is at pains to play off against Freud, originates in Ernst Mach's relativistic psychology. Like Musil and Malinowski (two other thinkers influenced by Mach), Canetti does not locate identity in a complex, layered psyche, but in the constantly shifting, frequently contradictory but always concrete manifestations of individual behaviour. In his English memoirs, Canetti tries to remain true to his impressions, even if they are ugly, and is *not* ashamed to expose his own faults. By the same logic he does not recoil from attacking his closest friends.

It is hardly surprising that a man of Canetti's stamp, although he met with affection in England for his human warmth, and admiration for his intellect, was rejected on many grounds—for his unconventional scholarship, his strongly held opinions, or just for his downright egotism. Unlike some émigrés, such as those who excelled in British academe, Canetti never deigned to adopt the requisite veneer of urbane gentility that might have won him universal acceptance. John Bayley's satirical epithet for him, "the godmonster of Hampstead", aptly betrays the problem. Paradoxically, the very tolerance Canetti encountered here enabled him to cultivate his idiosyncracies. No wonder that he came to regard himself as what he calls a "*liebender Engländer*", i.e. an Englishman by attachment, not birth.

Canetti frequently allows the reader to infer how much he owes his English friends intellectually. Arthur Waley's oriental studies, C. V. Wedgwood's historical work and Franz Steiner's social anthropology are among the sources he used in his own writings. Behind each of the friends in his memoirs there is an implicit library. This is obvious in the case of a celebrated poet and critic such as William Empson, but it holds good also for a less well-known figure such as Aymer Maxwell, who grew up with his grandfather, an ageing scholar and painter. Quite a few of the scholars Canetti introduces were from distinguished backgrounds, and several were leading authorities in their field. His choices suggest the link between class, culture and politics that typified the 1940s and '50s.

To understand Canetti's argument in full, one would need to read his friends' books. For example, his favourites among Waley's translations hint at sympathies that Canetti never verbalises explicitly. The poems by Po Chü-I which he refers to recall Canetti's own political views. The brief poem "A Protest in the Sixth Year of Ch'ien Fu" reads like a crystallisation of Canetti's thoughts, seeming to anticipate his theses in *Crowds and Power*:

> *The hills and rivers of the lowland country*
> *You have made your battleground.*
> *How do you suppose the people who live there*
> *Will procure "firewood and hay"?*
> *Do not let me hear you talking together*
> *About titles and promotions;*
> *For a single general's reputation*
> *Is made out of ten thousand corpses.*

Po Chü-I exhibits an exceptional grasp of the structures that connect crowds and power, hierarchies and death, and social distinctions and exploitation. In his biography, *The Life and Times of Po Chü-I*, which appeared in 1949, Waley relates the poet's views to his life. In the year 844 Po Chü-I proposed securing the banks of a river that had cost the lives of many sailors and porters:

> *Ships and barges when passing through this point frequently*

capsized and were damaged or destroyed. Often in the depth
of winter the cries of the sailors or coolies harnessed to the
boats, who had been flung into the freezing water barefoot
and scantily clad, could be heard all night. I had long been
determined, if it should ever be in my power to do so, to help
these unfortunate people . . .

The solution to this problem constitutes an ideal of social action in which community, rank and power are harmoniously united for the common good.

Canetti's closest friends in England were often in some sense outsiders. Many came from the Celtic fringe, others were Catholics or Quakers. Among these were Iris Murdoch, London Irish by birth; Kathleen Raine, whose religion inclined towards magic, and C. V. Wedgwood, who came from a Quaker family and experienced difficulties accommodating to English social life; then there were the Maxwells who had grown up in the Scottish Apostolic Church, and had their own problems as homosexuals. The close friendships Canetti enjoyed with these people, who were outsiders yet belonged to the Establishment, afforded him insights into English life such as few continental Europeans have been privileged to obtain.

Canetti adopts in the main the standpoint of a Hampstead intellectual—someone who is not taking part in the War, devotes himself to learning and culture, has little time for English country life, makes the obligatory trip to Scotland, and knows England chiefly as a cosmopolitan city dweller. He really makes no distinction between London and England, and has no feeling for the counties, let alone their differences. It is hardly surprising, therefore, that when he describes his journey to Scotland, his narrative sounds like a tale by Evelyn Waugh; whereas the embarrassing episode with the diamonds reads like a moment in Henry James. "England's green and pleasant land", so central to the English myth, seems not to interest Canetti at all. On the other hand, he does draw an implicit connection with the idea of a "new Jerusalem" when describing the Anglican cemetery in Church Row in Hampstead in terms that recall a traditional Jewish graveyard.

His method is painterly. He leaves many well-known facts unsaid, as if placing them in the background, while emphasising others, to make them stand out in a new light. When the English characterise England, they think of things like Parliament and the class system, tolerance and justice, town and country, food and weather, football and cricket, and the control of personal feelings. Canetti knows all that, but he takes a different line. He wants to draw new distinctions, pursue hidden links. Instead of dwelling on class, which plays so large a part in English self-understanding, he notes a caste system typified by subtly differentiated hierarchies. Caste pride is expressed in English arrogance. Instead of unravelling the history of the English attitude to feeling, he tries to capture its modern variant, and relate this to English society as he finds it. Above all, though—and here too one recognises the author of *Crowds and Power*—he seems interested in finding the archetype or model of English society. For Canetti, the essence of English social life lies in the *party*.

He must have been a frequent party-goer to judge by the well-informed distaste of his recollections. His German term for these English gatherings, *Nichtberührungsfeste*, is utterly untranslatable: an exact version like "ritualised celebrations of non-contact" cannot help but miss the witty pungency of Canetti's term. The idea recalls the opening chapter of *Crowds and Power*, which treats what Canetti there calls *Berührungsfurcht*, the fear of physical contact, as a starting point for his investigation. The parties he has in mind are a relatively recent invention, and derive from the "cocktail parties" of the '30s. In Canetti's day, they were central to social life, and literary parties were an essential part of the scene.

This must have been hard to stomach for a Central European intellectual addicted to coffee-house culture. The refugees tried to recreate their lost world in the much lamented Cosmo in Finchley Road. Canetti's favourite café was the Coffee Cup in Hampstead, which is still there today. Visiting it now, it is hard to imagine Canetti holding court here for his younger friends. As Gavin Maxwell recalled, he was their "master", and "sage", a modern Socrates who gathered his disciples about him. Although this is how some of his English friends best remember him, in his memoir Canetti makes no attempt to recreate his own café life or that of the émigrés in general. He doesn't have much time for pubs, either—he presumably knew his way around Fitzrovia, since this is where he met with Dylan Thomas. The only pub he describes is the rather exclusive establishment in Downshire Hill.

Setting aside pubs and cafés enables Canetti to concentrate on parties. Practically every larger gathering he describes can be understood as a form of party—not just the obvious ones in Hampstead but the dinner parties, too, and even the country-house party in Scotland or the trip to Marrakesh in 1954 with Aymer and his friends, which was a sort of travelling party. Canetti never tries to link the parties in the '40s and '50s with the party political system, but one cannot help but wonder whether he is not hinting at a connection. In treating the party as the English social form par excellence he may well be hinting at a link between social and political life.

In Canetti's day people threw parties and held dinner parties for every conceivable occasion. Diana Spearman, a hostess of the kind to whom Canetti felt particularly drawn, had the means to entertain a remarkable circle of intellectuals and politicians at her home in Lord North Street. She was a wealthy divorcée, dressed in the finest in haute couture, and worked at the Conservative Party Research Department. She enjoyed a reputation as a writer, and broke new ground with her book on the sociology of the novel. We may suppose that she consciously staged the meeting between Canetti and Enoch Powell described in these memoirs. On another occasion she introduced Karl Popper to Powell. According to Mary Douglas, Popper had told Spearman that Powell's poetry reminded him of Goethe, and the Tory hostess wanted him to repeat the compliment in Powell's hearing. Things did not quite work out. Powell occasioned Popper some embarrassment by asking him which particular Goethe poem he had in mind. On another occasion, Spearman (who worked in the same office as James Douglas, Mary Douglas' husband) organised a dinner to introduce Canetti to Mary Douglas, who had recently published a piece on the hunting practices of the Lele, an African tribe that had much impressed Canetti. He picks up the theme in his discussion of hunting in *Crowds and Power*. A friendship developed, and Mary Douglas invited him to her own dinner parties. At one of these she rehearsed the theories of *Purity and Danger*, and Canetti showed a ready grasp of her new theory—understandably, given the importance of his friend Franz Steiner's book on *Taboo* for the development of her ideas. She later introduced Canetti to her students at a Hampstead pub, and Canetti also attended a student Christmas party in her department at University College, London. However, she avoided speaking about *Crowds and Power*, a work for which she had little taste. The last time she saw him was at a farewell gathering that some of his friends had organised for him somewhere in Hampstead. He was about to leave England for Zurich for good. By now, he was no longer an obscure émigré but a Nobel laureate, and the anxieties caused by his lack of recognition as a writer had been replaced by those he experienced as a celebrity.

The long trail of Canetti's struggle for recognition and his anger at the English literary establishment is nowhere more apparent than in his grotesque account of the party attended by T. S. Eliot and Dylan Thomas. The scene he evokes symbolises the wider conflicts he detects in English life with their differences between London and the provinces, the English and the Celts, the right and the left, and between emotional coldness and genuine feelings. The references to the Civil War in the memoirs indicate that Canetti must have been aware that the contrasts ultimately echo the conflict between Roundheads and Cavaliers, and we may suppose that Eliot also represented the Anglican Church in his eyes, a religion in which he evinces no interest whatsoever. His allegiance is with Blake, with nonconformism, with the sects and heresies. Everything that Canetti hates about his beloved England thus seems to be embodied in Eliot's character.

He doesn't bother with analyses—whether of his own gripes or of Eliot's motives. He makes no attempt to understand the great poet. He simply abuses him, without asking whether his insults are socially acceptable or not. His abreaction constitutes the greatest possible contrast to the culture that—according to Canetti—Eliot represents, the culture of emotional coldness. He could have attacked Eliot's anti-Semitism, or he could have taken Eliot to task for his published views on the need for tolerance towards the Nazis. But Canetti does not argue with Eliot's ideas. Instead, he takes on the whole man, both his life and his work.

The better to understand the ferocity of Canetti's attitude it is worth considering some of the layers that made up his own personality: his Eastern European background in Bulgaria; the Talmudic argumentation developed in the Jewish schools, sharp, unbending, and uncompromising in manner; the cognate, often inflexible attitudes displayed by the Central European intellectual on points of principle; Karl Kraus' satire on the enemies of civilisation; and finally perhaps Shaftesbury's concept of "the whole man" proclaimed by Goethe and Schiller that was reactivated by Hofmannsthal and others in Vienna, an ideal of wholeness that both in the *Sturm und Drang* and latter-day Vienna contributed to the stripping away of hypocrisy. In many ways, these traditions converged in ideas of being human that were the very antithesis of English life, and for Canetti it seems that T. S. Eliot epitomised this difference.

Eliot's friend John Hayward, a man for whom Canetti shows scant affection, had proclaimed Eliot to be a critic in the same class as Dryden, Johnson and Coleridge: if Canetti wanted to achieve a similar place on the English scene—a somewhat implausible ambition for a German-speaking writer—this therefore was the man to attack. In writing the English memoirs, Canetti unwittingly rehearses his earlier battles for acceptance, projecting the anguished frustrations of the exile onto the culture hero, the intellectual embodiment of the host nation.

Canetti's allusions to Eliot's works help to explain his attitude. When he refers to Eliot's thinking on Blake, he is probably thinking about the way in which Eliot normalises Blake's poetry in his essay, a reading that somehow reduces Blake's originality (one can imagine Canetti cringing at Eliot's conclusion: "the peculiarity is seen to be *the peculiarity of all great poetry.*"); when he criticises Eliot's view of Dante he must be thinking of "What Is a Classic?", a text that praises Dante as the creator of a new language, whereas Canetti would no doubt have regarded him as the supreme poet of Hell; and finally, when Canetti reproaches Eliot for his questionable attitude to Goethe (the greatest of all the poets in the eyes of both Canetti and Veza), he must be thinking about the fact that when Eliot first wrote about Goethe, he had denied the German poet's greatness, changing his mind only on receiving the well-endowed Goethe Prize. Canetti, who refused to work on commission, hated the fact that Eliot wrote plays for money.

Canetti spices his memoirs with some fine phrases, and the new word *Gefühlsimpotenz* (emotional impotence) he coins, with which to abuse the English, is no exception. As a dig at the marital problems that were rife in English society, this is below the belt; but as a formula for the affective deficits of English life, it could hardly be bettered. Intriguingly, Canetti links this much-noted deficiency to the virtue of tolerance: the same elements of English life that promote fairness in the social sphere, according to Canetti, lead to deep inter-personal problems.

His refusal to be fair in a conventional way, then, goes together with his emphasis on the emotions. He is interested in emotional facts, not historical facticity. Considering that it was Eliot who defined the "dissociation of sensibility"—which is, essentially, what Canetti accuses him of suffering from—the criticism of Eliot may be ignoble, but it forms a necessary part of Canetti's corrective vision. For Canetti, Eliot is both the greatest poet of his age and a parvenu, an immigrant who became a symbol of the host nation by adopting its historical characteristics in an extreme form. Whereas Eliot embraced the device of assimilation, Canetti rejects it utterly. Like Eliot, though, Canetti has a visitor's eye for the historical *longue durée*.

He is fascinated by the links between the Thirty Years War and the English Revolution, and by the way in which the battles of the Civil War continue in the power struggles of the literary avant-garde. Yet he does not for a moment consider the possibility that Eliot might actually have been a victim of his historical situation.

Canetti's capacity for love, which is so winningly drawn in Kathleen Raine's autobiography *The Lion's Mouth*, stood in sharp contrast with his individualism. The tensions that arose from this conflict might have torn him apart had he not hit upon the principle of transformation. It was this, presumably, which saved him from destroying himself. He is the man he loves. Ultimately, he is the one he hates. It is easy to criticise his views. Understanding him is more difficult.

His manner of throwing things into relief or exaggerating the contrast between light and shade like some literary Caravaggio can be disconcerting. On occasion, though, it is possible to detect a principle of distributive justice behind his technique, notably in his treatment of the Maxwell brothers and Kathleen Raine. She describes her passion for Gavin in *The Lion's Mouth*, a book which generously recalls Canetti's role as a counsellor. He had warned her that her love was hopeless, and tried to save his friends from the worst when the affair took a tragic turn. Gavin likewise recognised Canetti's help, writing about it in an autobiographical text quoted by his biographer, Douglas Botting. However, when Botting wanted to learn more about the affair from Canetti, Canetti refused to provide any further information. Gavin had not given him permission to tell a third party. If Canetti's attitude towards Kathleen Raine was unfair, it was probably motivated by the wish to be fair to Gavin, who, on her own admission, had suffered so much at her hands. In general, though, Canetti tends to be harsher on women—Iris,

C. V. Wedgwood, Margaret Thatcher—than on his male friends.

For all the difference between himself and the Maxwells, Canetti sees their relationship as a kind of elective affinity. Like Canetti, the Maxwells had lost their father at a tender age. In his English memoirs, Canetti corrects the inequality between the brothers—the younger Gavin was far more glamorous than his elder brother—by attributing some of the qualities we associate with Gavin to Aymer. Gavin and Aymer both drove fast cars and indulged in motor racing. Gavin's driving was notorious and, as Douglas Botting observes, Gavin liked to remember a conversation with Canetti about it on their drive to Scotland:

> *"Gavin, Gavin," Gavin gleefully mimicked Canetti's English accent, "do you really have to identify with a motor car in this way? I mean, when the car goes fast, do you feel fast? When it goes slow, do you feel slow? When it breaks down, do you feel broken down?" "Yes, all of those things."*

In his memoirs, however, Canetti writes only about Aymer's driving. In making his little monument for Aymer, his friend and long-standing patron, it is ironic that Canetti should define the scion of one of Britain's oldest families with what is according to the Futurists the central attribute of modernity, namely "speed". It would be worth pursuing these links between Canetti and the Maxwells. After travelling in North Africa, Gavin wrote his *Lords of the Atlas*, an account of a modern despot who closely conforms to a type that Canetti analyses in *Crowds and Power*; and for his part Canetti wrote his only travel book after his journey to North Africa, *The Voices of Marrakesh*, the work that first brought him to the attention of a wider audience. How much did Canetti's concept of despotism contribute to Gavin's book? What role did Maxwell play in Canetti's only anthropological "field trip"? These questions are typical of the many issues raised by Canetti's relations with his English friends.

Canetti's life in England would have been unimaginable without Veza. Although she does appear—for example, in Canetti's description of life at Amersham and in his anecdote about her embarrassing meeting with Arthur Waley—he never says exactly what she meant to him. The memory of her seems to have been too painful for him to attempt a portrait. To complete the account of his English years, one would have to add a fuller picture of Veza—her wit, her sharp tongue, her fiery nature, her suffering, her compassion for the suffering of others, especially women. Above all, one would have to write about her novels and stories: nobody reading these memoirs could guess that Veza and Canetti enjoyed a literary partnership that lasted more than 30 years. But what can one say? It was such a complicated relationship that any comment seems intrusive.

Veza tolerated Canetti's idiosyncracies, knew his mistakes, encouraged his gifts, and shielded him from the world. They spoke Ladino, the Spanish dialect that their ancestors had taken with them into exile, and this shared language no doubt contributed to their bond. They even spoke it in company like a secret code, which made it all the harder for an outsider to gain an insight into their relationship. (My understanding that Canetti's Ladino was perfect is contradicted by Helder Macedo, who noted some grammatical inaccuracies in his speech.) Veza was certainly proud of her position as Canetti's wife, but accepted his other relationships. "Canetti can have as many women as he wants," she would say, "but there is only one Mrs Canetti." She also enjoyed good relationships with some of his mistresses, evidenced by some joke photographs she took with Marie-Louise von Motesiczky at Amersham. In one, Veza is seated before *The Spanish Lady*, a portrait that she resembled, and Marie-Louise sits before her own *Self-Portrait in Red Hat*, a picture she gave to Canetti (but later took back). Iris Murdoch loved Veza, admiring her fighting spirit, which was never intimidated by Canetti: she knew how to control him with her sarcasm, and mocked his most deeply held *idées fixes* with impunity.

In a letter to a friend after her death, Canetti admitted that Veza's intellectual role in the writing of *Crowds and Power* had been as great as his own, and that he had discussed every word of the book with her. Readers cannot help but be struck by the similarity of their ideas, even by their stylistic affinities. With the publication of *Crowds and Power*, which she had worked so tirelessly to promote, and which he had finished as much thanks to her bullying and badgering as to his own obsession, her life's work was essentially done. In a moral sense, the book constituted the sacrifice that they made in return for their deliverance from the terrible fate of their people. With the book's publication, her life fulfilled its purpose; when she died, his own life also lost its meaning, and he came close to ending it. He confesses in the section of his English memoirs that deals with Church Row that he now renounced the views on cemeteries he had set out in *Crowds and Power*, adopting Veza's perspective instead. Her death in 1963 marked the beginning of the end of his English period. Now he was drawn to Zurich, where he was fortunate enough to be able to begin his life all over again. For a while he kept his flat in London and returned for occasional visits, but in the end he gave up his London home. Veza's discovery and posthumous fame as a writer belong to Canetti's Zurich period, and have no place in this book. When her novel, *Yellow Street*, first appeared in German in 1990, she at last emerged from the shadows to take her rightful place beside her husband as a major writer. Nobody was more pleased than Canetti.

The points where Canetti seems harsh cannot be overlooked. Those where he corrects injustice or atones for his failings are less obvious. The portrait of Franz Steiner is a case in point. In the 1940s Steiner was Canetti's closest literary friend. They had much in common and there are many parallels between their work. Both saw themselves as "orientals" in the West; both were researching for major studies dedicated to opposing dictatorship, Canetti on crowd phenomena, Steiner on slavery; both regarded their work as a form of sacrifice; both, as Canetti recalls, were devoted to myth; and both turned to the aphorism as a favoured genre during the War, Canetti from 1942, Steiner (following his example) from 1943. Canetti once misguidedly accused Steiner of plagiarism and temporarily broke with him. Steiner, who admired Canetti's brilliance, must have owed his slightly older friend a good deal: his reflections on death can perhaps only be fully grasped in the context of Canetti's thinking. But there is strong evidence that the influence went both ways. For instance, Steiner's idea of the poet, or *Dichter*, as a "guardian of the myths of every people", formulated in 1943, reappears 30 years later in Canetti's celebrated characterisation of the writer as the "guardian of metamorphosis". Canetti's portrait of his friend, without actually acknowledging such debts, goes a long way towards effecting moral recompense by the depth of its homage to Steiner's intellect.

In honouring his memory, Canetti also cuts a lance for Steiner's poetry. Steiner shared Canetti's attitude towards Eliot, albeit with more ambiguities: he abhorred Eliot's anti-

Semitism while acknowledging his mastery as a poet, and consciously adapted the form of *Four Quartets* in his own *magnum opus*, the *Conquests*. Yet if Steiner's verse enacted an eloquent tribute to Eliot, he nonetheless rounded on him in a parody that ranges from wry amusement to outright bitterness, attacking the English poet's montage of quotations, his social stance, and, as Steiner saw it, his shallow response to the War:

Of Sleeping draughts or dreaming draughts . . .

Sometimes Homer nods, sometimes Freud dreams,
But Mr Eliot sometimes speaks
Of sleeping draughts or waking draughts,
Of sleeping draughts or dreaming draughts,
For life is very draughty,
But thus, and not otherwise, behind barred quotations,
When time passes.

Oh, wherever you may be, playing chess or whistling
A waste *ländler* at Cannae or Guernica:
Among the one-eyed at times a blind man is king,
L'état c'est moi.

For both Steiner and Canetti, two émigré outsiders, Eliot represented the archetypal insider. With remarkable ferocity, Canetti nursed his resentment of Eliot's power for almost half a century until he, like Eliot, had become a Nobel laureate, a grand old man of modern letters. Yet Steiner missed out. Exile and his untimely death prevented him from achieving literary recognition. That is an injustice Canetti sets right in treating him as a thinking man devoted to myth; and by singling out his poem, "Prayer in the Garden", he draws attention to a neglected masterpiece—one of the few valid poetic responses to the Shoah. To fully understand Canetti's spleen against Eliot, therefore, one would first need to immerse oneself in Steiner's apotheosis of suffering.

The memoirs chiefly cover the first ten to twenty years of Canetti's emigration, focusing on the time before *Crowds and Power* was published in 1960. The first sections of *Party in the Blitz*, notably the recollections of Amersham, seem very much the product of his memories of the cold, stiff, formal social world he entered upon his arrival. However, the last sections to be written, which include the critical passages on T. S. Eliot and Iris Murdoch, seem to have been influenced by his negative reaction to Margaret Thatcher and the Falklands War. His rage against what he regards as the English emotional coldness of the 1940s becomes curiously contaminated with his anger at Thatcherism. The resulting perspective is slightly odd, not to say confused. The strength of what Canetti here has to say is perhaps his recognition of an unsavoury link between the ideological aberrations of the 1930s and '40s and the dubious tendencies of the '80s and '90s—a parallel perhaps indicated by the current fascination with the Weimar Republic and the popularity of a writer like Joseph Roth. But as Canetti did not live to complete his book, he was never able to develop the parallels between Fascism and Armani Fascism and between Communism and market Maoism in any convincing way.

Canetti's view of England oscillates between that of a neutral traveller and that of a cultural critic. Sometimes, one has the feeling that a latter-day Karl Kraus has turned his eyes on the Island Race. But then again, even with a writer as concrete and resistant to theory as Canetti, one can't help but note certain continental habits, such as a tendency to essentialise races and peoples. He has a fondness for bundling together phenomena that on closer inspection might prove to be entirely unconnected.

There is a certain grim satisfaction in his tone when he rehearses the old argument that England had given its best in the Second World War and was now in the grip of decline. Is he upset, or does his belief give him some perverse pleasure? He tries to link this supposed decline with his view of Enoch Powell and Thatcherism, but the point seems forced. He exaggerates Enoch Powell's success, and forgets that after the "rivers of blood" speech Enoch Powell's career reached a dead-end. England did not support him in the way that Canetti thinks, certainly not in the long term, and tended to reassert the more tolerant, liberal attitudes that had welcomed Canetti and so many other refugees in the 1930s. Perhaps he is on safer ground with Margaret Thatcher, but even here one senses that his antagonism has a wilful streak more connected to his own dislike of women in power and his proclivity for conflict—with Thatcher and other public figures such as Iris Murdoch—than with a rounded view of the case. Canetti certainly has an eye for the faults of the *me* generation (albeit the yuppies did not wear pinstripes), but he seems unaware of the change in attitude to the emotions that set in around that time. The public grief over the death of Diana, Princess of Wales, shows that England was moving in directions that Canetti knew nothing about. He seems quite unaware of the new "touchy feely" phenomenon, the kissing, hugging, touching, crying and confessing of late twentieth-century England. In fact, the emotional reversal that occurred in the '80s and '90s, integrating the continental cult of feeling into English life, probably owed a lot to the gradual assimilation of the pre-war immigrants from continental

Europe of whom Canetti himself was a prime example.

Yet Canetti was certainly right about one thing. The revolution of the Thatcher years spelled the end of *his* England. The reign of the Hampstead intellectuals was over.

Just as Canetti links his arrival to the historical caesura of the Second World War, he wants to connect his departure to another historical rift. This is partly to dramatise his own importance, partly as structural tool in building his narrative, and partly for satirical purposes, in order to attack morals and manners. Like Swift, whom he loved for his ability to hate, Canetti is in Richard Ellman's telling phrase "a mad egoist", and imagines a past made up of "sweetness and light" in order to attack the "dirt and poison" of the present. A true admirer of Swift, he satirises England with all the means at his disposal— exaggeration, mockery, distortion—to make a wider moral point.

He enjoys his ambiguous love–hate relationship with his adoptive home, and this is reflected in his no less difficult relationships with his friends.

Canetti's capacity for friendship, his ability to listen, and his readiness to help were so strongly developed, and he dispensed them with such reckless generosity, that to preserve his own identity his best qualities would often go into reverse, as it were transforming into their own opposite, and become a grotesque caricature of his better nature. Then indeed the "god" became a "monster". He would stop listening. Refuse to help. Disappear—as he does in one of Iris Murdoch's novels. Veza summed him up with a quote from Goethe: "Where there is much light, there is much shade."

Nowhere do his feelings about England and the complexities of his character become clearer than in his devastating pictures of Iris Murdoch. We know how highly he regarded Iris, and he alludes to that opinion in his portrait of their mutual friend, Franz Steiner. In German he uses the word *Dichter* for her. It means both poet and writer, and is the term he elaborates in his essay "The Writer's Profession" in order to explain his calling. He normally reserves the word for the writers he reveres— figures like Kraus, Musil and Broch. Even in deriding Iris as an "*illegitimen Dichter*", then, I think he recognises her talent. He turns her into a counter-image of his own self, attacking her with unrestrained ferocity, dismembering every thread of her being. Everything in his portrait remains poised, of a terrible composure. Every word seems to quiver with rage.

The attack recalls the diatribes of the Reformation pamphleteers or the unflinching gaze of a clinical portrait painter. Mindful of this analogy, with an inspirational comparison he cites Memling when evoking her skin, but he also borrows Marie-Louise's sharp eye—she once did a cruelly unflattering portrait of Iris—and concludes by representing Iris as a clumsy Brueghel peasant, a bitter reference to their meeting in the gallery where the Brueghels are hung at the Kunsthistorisches Museum in Vienna. When it comes to describing Iris' blouse, it is Aymer Maxwell's eyes that Canetti borrows. This layering of references makes his portrait of Iris more cunning, and even more allusive than his attack on Eliot.

He presents her as his polar opposite, objectifying his own character in his sketch. Partly because of the shock effect, which not even repeated readings can diminish, and partly because of the curious perspective, which mingles his own qualities with Iris', it is impossible to consider the piece objectively. It reads in part like a satirical inversion of Canetti's own nature: the many novels she wrote provide a foil to the cycle of eight he never completed; and her philosophical *magnum opus*, *Metaphysics as a Guide to Morals*, which provides the occasion for his rant, serves as the intellectual opposite of *Crowds and Power*. He seems unaware that her book was directed against the very forces that were rampant in the Thatcher years that so upset him, that Iris' rehabilitation of goodness as a philosophical concept in a hostile world provided a major attempt to resolve these problems, and that if anything *Metaphysics as a Guide to Morals* tried to create an admittedly late-twentieth-century parallel to *Crowds and Power* as a book designed to change the way that human beings act. He does not see its qualities, only its scholastic method, its turgid style, its medley of references—symptomatic is her unthinking naming of Canetti in the same breath as Freud—and her kowtowing to authority, what Canetti takes to be her refusal to be herself. The painterly technique he uses for his critique, then, exploits an unusual angle, involving a fragmentation reminiscent of the Cubists. In depicting Iris, Canetti the autobiographer actually discloses elements of his own inner nature. The evil, the baseness of which a human being is capable, does not reside in Iris, the Platonic seeker after the Good, but in the eye of the beholder, Elias Canetti himself. Indeed, his criticisms only make sense as a self-portrait, in that his attack proves to be what Goethe said about his own writing: a fragment of a great confession.

In Michael Hofmann, Canetti has found an ideal translator, who through his advocacy and translations of Joseph Roth is as familiar with Canetti's cultural home, the Austro-Hungarian Empire, as he is with his second home, Britain: he knows London's émigré world, its wider literary scene, its Hampstead scenery, and brings a poet's sensitivity to his task. He sees the redemptive vigour, the joy in Canetti's writing, even when Canetti is at his most rancorous, and has found the *mot juste* and an English voice for the life that lifts this book far above the often stormy emotions in which it originated.

Jeremy Adler
King's College
London

A NOTE ON THE TEXT

The papers of the Elias Canetti Estate included the following fragments of a book on his English years:

A.: A shorthand manuscript written in October 1990 and continued in January and November 1991.

B.: A largely shorthand manuscript written in July and August 1992. This is the main body of material. The texts from A. are mostly incorporated in this version.

C.: A number of notes and diaries written in February–April and August–November 1993 including passages on England. Composed largely in shorthand. Apart from passages that Canetti explicitly classified as "Diaries" and are not to be published until thirty years after his death, this contains two groups of fragments on England: the continuation of his individual portraits and a continuous text that widens out and summarises the book.

D.: A typescript copy of approximately the first half of the texts from B. that Canetti dictated to his daughter Johanna in 1994 on the basis of his shorthand manuscripts.

After Canetti's death, at the request of Johanna Canetti, Florindo Tarreghetta transcribed A., B. and C. This transcription provided the basis for *Party im Blitz: Die englischen Jahre.*

Following the German original, the present edition begins with the most recently written part: the second half of C. (pp. 1-24). This is followed by a section from A. (pp. 25-31) and the printing of B. (pp. 32-160). This represents the most thoroughly developed section of the project. Canetti described it as "a provisional, unsorted version." The original editor Kristian Wachinger of the German publisher Hanser in Munich prepared the text and has placed the sections into a logical order, referring to A. and D. for the correction of errors. Additional passages were included from A.: pp. 56-57; p. 62, lines 1–17; p.66, lines 13–16; and p. 114. The large piece on Franz Baermann Steiner (pp. 115-121) was first published posthumously in *Akzente* 3/1995 (and reprinted in Elias Canetti: *Aufzeichnungen 1992–1993*, Munich 1996): that text is based on a manuscript that Canetti wrote at Jeremy Adler's suggestion for a special edition of *Akzente* devoted to Steiner in 1992. Ignoring the requests of his long-time editor Michael Krüger, Canetti did not release it for publication during his lifetime, and it first appeared posthumously in 1995. The volume concludes with the first half of C. (pp. 161-194).

This publication would not have been possible without the generous help of Johanna Canetti. Thanks for assistance and additional research are also due to Julia Breimeier in Munich, Roberto Calasso in Milan, Sven Hanuschek in Munich, Susanne Hornfeck in Munich, Jill Lloyd in London, Peter von Matt in Zurich and Hans Reiss in Bristol. Several readers sent in corrections to the first German edition. These have, gratefully, been incorporated into the English version by the editors of The Harvill Press, London, New Directions' British co-publisher of *Party in the Blitz*.

LIST OF ILLUSTRATIONS

Heath Street, Hampstead
(Carl Hanser Verlag Archive, Munich)

Friedl Benedikt
(Elias Canetti Estate, Zurich)

Veza Canetti in Marie-Louise von Motesiczky's studio in Amersham;
the painting on the stool to her left is a self portrait of Marie-Louise
von Motesiczky
(Elias Canetti Estate, Zurich)

Mrs Milburn, Amersham
(Elias Canetti Estate, Zurich)

Anne's Corner, Chesham Bois
(Carl Hanser Verlag Archive, Munich)

Elias Canetti in Scotland, 1951
(Elias Canetti Estate, Zurich)

On the monastery island at Mochrum, 1950
(Elias Canetti Estate, Zurich)

Aymer Maxwell
(Elias Canetti Estate, Zurich)

Franz Baermann Steiner
(Deutsches Literaturarchiv, Marbach)

Keats' House, Wentworth Place, Hampstead
(Carl Hanser Verlag Archive, Munich)

Elias Canetti on Hampstead Heath
(Stern/picture press—Photo: Meffert)

Iris Murdoch (Taken by Franz Steiner)
(Jeremy Adler, London)

Clement Glock
(Elias Canetti Estate, Zurich)

Elias Canetti in Hampstead Cemetery
(Stern/picture press—Photo: Meffert)

NOTES

1 *Heath*: Hampstead Heath, North London. Frequented during the nineteenth century by poets including Coleridge and Keats. Situated in its immediate vicinity are Downshire Hall, 8 Thurlow Road (Canetti's principal residence into the 1960s and second home until 1988),and Keats' House.

2 *Burton*: Robert Burton (1577–1640), priest, author (*The Anatomy of Melancholy*, 1621).—*Sir Thomas Browne*: (1605–82), physician, author (*Religio Medici*, 1643; *Vulgar Errors*, 1646; *Urn Burial*, 1658). —*John Aubrey*: (1626–97), antiquary, author (posthumously: *The Natural History and Antiquities of Surrey*, 1719; *Lives of Eminent Men*, 1813 — a later selection of which endures as *Brief Lives*). — *George Fox*: (1624–91), founder of the Society of Friends (the Quakers). —*Hobbes*: Thomas Hobbes (1588–1679), philosopher, author (*Corpore Politico*, 1650; *Leviathan*, 1651; and *De Homine*, 1658). —*Laforgue:* Jules Laforgue (1860–1887), French poet. *Auto da Fé*: Elias Canetti's novel *Die Blendung* was published in Vienna in 1935 and in an English translation by C. V. Wedgwood as *Auto da Fé* (or *Tower of Babel* in its American edition) in 1946.

3 *Canetti's addresses* in London were, in chronological order: 31 Hyde Park Gardens (W2), 118 King Henry's Road (NW3), 14 Crawford Street (W1), 8 Thurlow Road (NW3).

4 *Empson:* William Empson (1906–1984), authoritative critic, poet, and author (*Seven Types of Ambiguity* 1930).

5 *Arthur Waley*: (1889–1966), poet, pre-eminent scholar of Asian literature, translator of Chinese poetry as well as *The Tale of Genji*.

6 *Kathleen Raine*: (1908–2003), poet, author, scholar of Coleridge and Blake, founder of *Temenos* magazine. —*John Hayward*: (1905–65), publisher, editor, and bibliophile.

7 *Amersham*: 30 miles northwest of London in the county of Buckinghamshire.

8 *Franz Steiner:* Franz Baermann Steiner (1909–52), poet and ethnologist. —*Kae Hursthouse*: fiancée of Franz Steiner, she took German lessons from Canetti in 1940. —*Student Movement House*: founded in 1917 in memory of students killed during the First World War; see also p. 169. —*L. H. Myers:* (1881–1944), author (*The Root and*

the Flower). —*Philip Toynbee*: (1916–81), novelist and journalist. —
Putnam publishers: Constant Davis Huntington (1876–1962), publisher of G. P. Putnam's Sons, London. *Alfreda*: Alfreda
Huntington (b. 1922), married to Brian Urquart. —*Yalta:* Villa
"Yalta" at Tiefenbrunnen, where Canetti lived as a boy in 1919,
while attending a girls' boarding school in Zürich: a situation (as
the only boy in a school full of girls) described in the first volume
of his autobiography, *The Tongue Set Free,* as a "paradise."

9 *Ernst Gombrich:* (1909–2001), Austro-British art historian, author
of the enormously successful *A Story of Art* (1950). —*I had a wife*:
Veza Canetti, née Venetiana Taubner-Calderon (1897–1963),
author (*Yellow Street* and *The Tortoises*).

10 *for five years now:* Canetti had kept the flat at 8 Thurlow Road until
1988 and spent several months a year there.

11 *I. A. Richards*: (1893–1979), critic and author (*Principles of Literary
Criticism*, 1921; *Practical Criticism*, 1928), collaborated with C. K.
Ogden on *The Meaning of Meaning, 1923*).

12 *Friedl*: Friedl Benedikt (1916–53), emigrated 1939, published three
novels, all dedicated to Canetti: see Canetti's *The Play of the Eyes.*

16 *Aymer*: Aymer Maxwell (1911–87), helped Canetti financially, went
on several long trips with him, including to Marrakesh in 1954: see
Canetti's *Voices of Marrakesh*, 1978. —*Gavin:* Gavin Maxwell
(1914–68), traveler and author (*Ring of Bright Water*, 1960). —
Veronica Wedgwood: C(icely) V(eronica) Wedgwood (1910–97),
historian and author, 1951–7 president of English PEN.

17 *Leith Hill:* favorite place for outings near Guildford, Surrey. —
Jonathan Cape: (1879–1960), publisher. —*Isherwood:* Christopher
Isherwood (1904–86), poet and author (*The Berlin Stories, All the
Conspirators*).

19 *Francis Galton:* (1822–1911), scientist, cousin of Darwin, founder of
eugenics. —*Leslie Stephen:* (1832–1904), ordained a priest, later a
critic. —*Diana Spearman*: author (*Modern Dictatorship*, 1939;
Democracy in England, 1957). *Maxwell-Fyfe*: David Maxwell-Fyfe
(Lord Kilmuir) (1900–67), lawyer, MP 1935–54, Lord Chancellor,
Solicitor-General, Home Secretary. —*Francis Graham-Harrison*:
(1914–2001), lifelong friend of Canetti, he married Carol Stewart
in 1941. —*Austin:* John Langshaw Austin (1911–60), Oxford
philosopher, author (*Philosophical Papers*, 1961; *Sense and Sensibilia*,

1962; *How to Do Things with Words,* 1962).

23 *a family of wine growers:* Canetti was probably introduced to the philosopher, sociologist, and musicologist Theodor W. Adorno (1903–69) by Marie-Louise von Motesiczky, who was related to him by marriage. In 1962 Adorno and Canetti conducted a celebrated radio discussion. —*Carol:* Carol Stewart (d. 2003) translator of Canetti's *Crowds and Power,* 1962.

27 *Mark Channing:* professional soldier in India, author (*Indian Mosaic,* 1936).

28 *Marie-Louise:* Marie-Louise von Motesiczky (1906–96), painter, pupil of Max Beckmann, emigrated to England in 1938, friend of Olda and Oskar Kokoschka, painted various portraits of Canetti.

31 *Dunne:* J. W. Dunne (1875–1949), engineer, pioneer of air travel, author (*An Experiment with Time,* 1927, *Time and Conways,* (1937).

32 *a great part in our lives:* On the Canettis' stay with the Milburns see also Veza Canetti's story "Toogoods oder das Licht" in Veza Canetti's *Der Fund. Erzählungen und Stücke.*

52 *Herbert Read:* (1893–1968), author, art historian, poet, critic, Professor of Fine Art, editor of the *Burlington Magazine,* 1933–39.

58 *Pierre Emmanuel:* (1916–84), poet, correspondent for French radio, 1969–71 President of International PEN. —*William Empson's "basement":* Haverstock Hill.

59 *Sonia Brownell:* Sonia Mary Brownell (1918–80), Connolly's assistant at Horizon, married George Orwell in 1949, shortly before his death.

60 *Cyril Connolly* (1903–74), critic, journalist, 1940–49 founding editor (with Stephen Spender) of the literary magazine *Horizon,* author (*The Rock Pool,* 1939; *The Unquiet Grave,* 1944).

62 *Paolozzi:* Eduardo Paolozzi, sculptor (b. 1924).—*Clement Glock:* painter of the Hampstead Group.

63 *Edwin Muir:* (1887–1959), author, jointly translated major works by Kafka with his wife Willa.

84 *Bertrand Russell:* (1872–1970), philosopher, mathematician, social reformer, author (*The Principles of Mathematics,* 1903; *Marriage and Morals,* 1929), winner of the Nobel Prize for Literature in 1950.

89 *Mr Pannikar:* Kavalam Madhava Pannikar (1895–1963), journalist, politician.

97 *Engel Lund:* (1900–66), Danish singer.

99 *Anna Mahler:* (1904–88), painter and sculptor, daughter of Gustav and Alma Mahler.

103 *Richard Law:* (1901–80), Minister of Education from 1945, created Lord Coleraine in 1954.

104 *Enoch Powell:* (1921–98), classical scholar, Conservative Member of Parliament 1950–74, Minister of Health 1960–3, opposed British entry to the Common Market, MP for the radical Ulster Unionists 1974–87, famously delivered a 1968 speech predicting that "rivers of blood" would flow in a future civil war between native Britons and immigrants.

107 *Montgomery:* Bernard Law Montgomery, 1st Viscount Montgomery of Alamein (1887–1967), commanded victorious Allied army over Rommel at Alamein, and was field commander of British troops during and after the Normandy landings.

110 *William the Silent:* William of Orange (1533–84), principal founder of Dutch independence and subject of C. V. Wedgwood's biography, *William the Silent: William of Nassau, Prince of Orange* (1960). —*Strafford:* Thomas Wentworth, Earl of Strafford (1593–1641), minister of Charles II and despotic Lord Deputy (Viceroy) of Ireland. —*Monmouth:* James Scott, Duke of Monmouth and Buccleugh (1649–86), led a rebellion after Charles II's death against his heir and brother, James II.

123 *Margaret:* Margaret Gardiner, wife of J. D. Bernal, author (*Barbara Hepworth. A Memoir*, 1982).

124 *Barbara Hepworth:* (1903–75), one of the leading exponents of British abstract sculpture, wife of Ben Nicholson, friend of Henry Moore.

126 *J. D. Bernal:* John Desmond Bernal (1901–71), scientist, politically active Communist, author (*Science in History*, 1954), husband of Margaret Gardiner.

129 *Geoffrey Pyke:* (1894–1948) incarcerated for espionage in the Ruhleben Camp during the WWI, author (*To Ruhleben—and Back*) after his escape. In 1939 organized an opinion poll which found that a majority of Germans opposed a war. —*Lord Mountbatten:* 1st Earl Mountbatten of Burma, Baron Romsey (1900–79), distinguished military career in the Second World War, last Viceroy of India, killed on board his yacht by an IRA bomb.

133 *Sir Henry Page Croft:* (1881–1947), MP 1918–1940. —*Fred Uhlman:* (1901–85), lawyer, painter, author, founder in 1938 of the Freier Deutscher Kulturbund at his home, 47 Downshire Hill. (He himself emigrated to Britain in 1936 for love of Diana Croft, and his émigrés' club for all opponents of Nazism who had fled to England was known in Britain as the FDKB; members included John Heartfield, Berthold Viertel and Stefan Zweig, Alfred Kerr and Oskar Kokoschka.)

134 *Stephen Spender:* (1909–95), poet, critic, publisher, translator (of Rilke's *Duino Elegies* with J. B. Leishman), ambulance driver in the Spanish Civil War, co-editor of *Horizon* with Cyril Connolly, and friend of T. S. Eliot and W. H. Auden. — *Oskar Kokoschka:* (1886–1980), Austrian painter and writer, fled to London from Vienna in 1938.

141 *Henry Moore:* (1898–1986), artist, moved in 1929 to Parkhill Road, Hampstead, with his Russian wife Irina and remained there until 1940, when the house was destroyed by a bomb. Thereafter they lodged at 21 Downshire Hill. —*Roland Penrose:* (1900–84), organized the 1936 International Surrealist Exhibition at his house, 21 Downshire Hill, already a rendezvous for artists, politicians and journalists. In 1947 founded the ICA (Institute of Contemporary Art) with Herbert Read and others. —*Lee Miller:* (1907–77), photographer for *Vogue*, war correspondent in Europe, photographed the liberation of the concentration camps at Buchenwald and Dachau.

150 *The Freemasons Arms:* 32 Downshire Hill.

151 *Mr Roberts:* George Roberts, James Joyce's editor at Maunsel & Co.

152 *Stevie Smith:* (1902–71), novelist (*Novel on Yellow Paper*), artist, poet (*Collected Poems; New Selected Poems*).

156 *Schiele:* Egon Schiele (1890–1918), Austrian painter.—*Loos:* Adolf Loos (1870–1933), Viennese architect.

157 *Hore-Belisha:* Leslie Hore-Belisha (1893–1957), successively Minister of Transport, War and Information, briefly Minister of National Insurance in 1945. Gave his name to the flashing yellow pedestrian crossing lights popularly known as "Belisha beacons."

160 *exhibition in the Städel:* exhibition at the Städel Museum, Frankfurt-am-Main, August 6–October 18, 1992. In July 1918 Kokoschka had commissioned the Munich doll-maker Hermina

Moos to produce a life-size doll of Alma Mahler to console him for his lost love; see Canetti's *The Play of the Eyes*, and *Oskar Kokoschka und Alma Mahler, Die Puppe—Epilog einer Passion*, exhibition catalog (Frankfurt, 1992).

161 *yesterday:* dated February 10, 1993.—*the thick philosophical tome*: Iris Murdoch, *Metaphysics as a Guide to Morals* (1992).

162 *these past forty years:* Canetti wrote this early in 1993; *Iris: A Memoir,* her husband John Bayley's account of her decline and death from Alzheimer's disease appeared in 1998.

163 *Simone Weil:* (1909–43), French philosopher, author, mystical Catholic.

174 *little volume on Sartre*: Iris Murdoch: *Sartre, Romantic Rationalist* (1953).

177 *Douglas Jay:* (1907–96), Labour Party politician, friend of Stephen Spender, cabinet minister in Harold Wilson's Labour government 1964–70, author (*The Socialist Case,* 1937; *Socialism in the New Society,* 1962). —*Ralph Vaughan Williams:* (1872–1958), composer, pupil of Max Bruch and Maurice Ravel, collector of folksongs, Professor at the Royal College of Music, London.

179 *Sonne:* Hebrew poet who published under the name of Avraham ben Yitshak; see Canetti's *Play of the Eyes.* —*Tales from Shakespeare:* prose versions of Shakespeare's plays by Charles and Mary Lamb (1807).

183 Morocco: see Canetti's *The Voices of Marrakesh.*

185 *The supreme preacher in the country was a woman:* Margaret Thatcher, Prime Minister 1979–90.

186 *a small war:* the Falklands War, 1982.

187 *a woman historian:* C. V. Wedgwood.

INDEX